SNOOP DOGG
REINCARNATED

PHOTOS BY WILLIE T. **SNOOP LION**

RIZZOLI
NEW YORK

New York · Paris · London · Milan

SNOOP DOGG

REINCA

RNATED

SNOOP LION

First published in the United States of America in 2013 by

Rizzoli International Publications, Inc.
300 Park Avenue South
New York, New York 10010
www.rizzoliusa.com

and

Vice Media Inc.
97 North Tenth Street
Brooklyn, New York 11211
www.vice.com

Designed by Stacy Wakefield

"La La La" from the LP *Reincarnated*
[C. Broadus, T. Pentz, A. Rechtshaid, J. Clarke, K. Boothe]
Executive Producer: Major Lazer
Berhane Sound System

SPECIAL THANKS TO:

H.I.M., Haile Selassie I, the Country and People of Jamaica, the Marleys, Haile Selassie I Theocratical Order of the Nyabinghi Reign, and the Writers and Musicians of *Reincarnated*

TEAM SNOOP: Ted Chung ★ Tiffany Chin ★ Kevin Barkey ★ Justin Li ★ Stampede Management ★ Cashmere Agency

TEAM VICE: Suroosh Alvi ★ Katie O'Neill ★ Andy Capper ★ Matt Schoen ★ Codine Williams

TEAM RIZZOLI: Leah Whisler, Editor ★ Kayleigh Jankowski ★ Colin Hough-Trapp, Production ★ Charles Miers, Publisher

2013 2014 2015 2016 2017 / 10 9 8 7 6 5 4 3 2 1

Printed in China
Conceived in Jamaica

Library of Congress Catalog Control Number: 2013937692

ISBN: 978-0-8478-4177-6

www.facebook.com/rizzolinewyork
www.facebook.com/snoopdogg
www.youtube.com/westfesttv
www.facebook.com/vice
www.youtube.com/vice

"I'm not The One nigga you could call me The Two / Bob Marley reincarnated, pupils dilated / Emancipated, concentrated, debated, rated many times / You surprised how I made it, huh? / You hate it, huh, but you know, I ain't even trippin' / I'm splittin' that Swisha up, plottin' on the come up."

—Snoop Dogg, "It Blows My Mind," 2003

"Niggas say smoke me out, yeah, I really doubt it / I'm Bob Marley reincarnated, so faded / So if you want it, you know yo' nigga, homie / You can put it in a Zag or a Blunt and get blunted."

—Snoop Dogg, "Kush," 2010

SERENDIPITY

Suroosh, left and Ted with Snoop, right.

★ **THE PRODUCERS OF** *REINCARNATED*–TED CHUNG (SNOOP'S MANAGER) AND SUROOSH ALVI (ONE OF THE FOUNDERS OF VICE)–SAT DOWN TO DISCUSS HOW THE PROJECT CAME TOGETHER.

TED CHUNG: During the summer of 2011, we were on the European leg of an international tour, and Snoop was thinking about the music direction for his next album. The discussion came up about finding a destination that would provide him the proper creative space–a place to take a break from his heavy touring and promotional schedule–to just have fun making music. There was so much going in our world at the time, both business and personal (much of which is covered in the documentary), and in a rare instance–the suggestion came up of us just going somewhere unique to record.

Snoop started talking about the genres of music he had explored throughout his career, and we noted how reggae and patois had a significant influence. The instinctive takeaway from this conversation was the idea of Jamaica as the isolated location we were looking for. My cursory thought at the time was: Jamaica has a strong musical history, beautiful landscape, and a cultural respect for smoking herb . . . all elements which should make for a comfortable creative atmosphere for Snoop. I could not have predicted how much more we would ultimately learn about Jamaica from the journey.

As Snoop brainstormed further, a particular lyric he had included in a few songs came to mind. Once, on the 2003 Neptunes album *Clones* in the song "It Blows My Mind," and again in the 2011 song "Kush" with Dr. Dre, Snoop makes casual reference to himself as "Bob Marley reincarnated" in the way MC's do when flexing their cultural relevance with lyrical dexterity. Since we were talking about Jamaica, creative dots connected, and the idea of the tentative project title "Reincarnated" was considered. It's significant how Snoop had put these rhymes out there in the hip-hop ethos, years before his trip to Jamaica, where they would assume a double . . . triple . . . quadruple entendre.

The rest of the project just fell into place serendipitously. Diplo has been a friend of the camp for a long time—and, via his Major Lazer projects, we knew Dip had experience with the musicians, producers, and studios of Jamaica. He heard about Snoop's plan and said, "Cool"—he was down to join the trip. Interestingly, Snoop's intial intent wasn't necessarily to focus on a reggae album per se; Diplo's a phenomenal producer for hip-hop, reggae, pop, and all genres. But, clearly, the *Reincarnated* experience guided Snoop and Major Lazer to focus on one mission.

Shortly thereafter for a separate marketing project, a trip to New York brought us by the Vice office. By chance, Snoop, crew, and I had just watched Vice's "Heavy Metal in Baghdad" on the tour bus in Europe, and Snoop loved how they were able to capture this interaction between underground music and global journalism with a unique perspective only Vice has. Personally, I've been a fan of the "Dos and Don'ts" section of the magazine, which was always really funny. We sat down at the office and Suroosh unexpectedly joined the meeting. I recognized Suroosh from a VBS TV video where he was shooting guns in Pakistan while interviewing arms dealers. I just started to think, "Okay, we're going to Jamaica—maybe someone should cover it . . . ." I threw out to him, "Hey, there's a chance we might be going to Jamaica for a month, potentially with Major Lazer. Would you guys be interested in documenting that?"

SUROOSH ALVI: I think when Ted came to the Vice offices, it was one of those things that just ended up in my schedule that said, "Meeting with Snoop Dogg's manager, Ted Chung," and I was kind of like, "What is this meeting?", and "Why am I going to this meeting with Snoop Dogg's manager?" I did a little bit of research on how the meeting came about, our respective teams decided that you and I should have a meeting. But I really went in with little expectation that anything was going to come of this, but I was excited at the prospect of meeting Snoop's manager. So I walked in and we just kind of stretched out and started talking, and an hour later we're still talking. Then Ted proposed this idea of, "maybe we could do this thing in Jamaica together," and it was on the heels of, I had spent the last two years deeply immersed in all the video production that this company had been doing. We had churned out a couple hundred hours of content in the two years leading up to when Ted and I met, and frankly, I was ready for a change. It had been very intense. And the idea of going to Jamaica to document something with Snoop was A) very different from all the other content we'd been creating, and B) it was also working with Snoop, which was really attractive on a lot of levels for our brand. And we had been having conversations at that time internally about the need for us to work with bigger artists for the benefit of our own brand profile, and there aren't that many artists that are a good fit, as well, and Snoop was one of these guys. I think when we were talking in that meeting, we noticed a lot of parallels and challenges that we deal with in our brand and that Snoop and you have to deal with, in terms of whether it's creating controversial content and navigating the brand world. We both push the envelope in our own ways and could instantly relate on that point.

And so I started getting excited about it and then we put some dates on the calendar, and from there we set up that meeting in LA where I came out to start mapping out the shoot, and also to meet with Snoop at his place in Hollywood. I was pretty nervous about that meeting, and not sure what to expect. And I think maybe Snoop needed to vet me as well. You needed to make sure Snoop was comfortable working with me. I got to see this really interesting

side of Snoop, which is the fact that he is an incredibly down-to-earth individual, and we were able to just bro down for a couple hours and have a great conversation, and the last thing he said to me at that meeting was, "Next time I see you, we'll be doin' it. It's on. I'll see you in Jamaica."

I personally got very involved in the project because I needed a change, the timing was perfect, and that led to us embarking on this journey together, the *Reincarnated* project, which on some level almost became a sabbatical from the type of work I'd been doing at Vice for the two years leading up to our trip to Jamaica.

TED: We called the Major Lazer camp, told them that this is happening for real, and it looked like Vice was joining us to document the trip. It started on a casual level because no one could have predicted what we were going to shoot in Jamaica or what the experience was for everyone involved. Diplo and team started doing their thing as far as calling in producers and writers. Keep in mind, since *Rhythm and Gangsta* with Pharrell, or I should say the Neptunes, we hadn't really gone in and done an album with one executive producer. There's usually a longer period of time to allow a project like that to gestate. Usually, everyone's in the States, and there's a comfort level. Being in Jamaica for a month and trying to see if there's music to be made or not . . . that's a whole different process to plan for. There was a handful of tracks Diplo had a chance to send over before going down. The one I remember which actually made the final record was an early demo of "Lighters Up." And like Suroosh said, this was going to be a very different production for all of us. Snoop's fans worldwide trust the creativity and honesty of his music, and, at this particular point in time as the film reveals, there were some things he was considering creatively he wanted to get off his chest that maybe he hadn't had a chance to on his past albums—and *Reincarnated* was the project to do just that.

That's when there started to be a recognition of where Snoop would take us on this journey—and he said, "Call Vice and tell them to meet us in Jamaica . . . let's record moments before I leave Los Angeles. If I'm going to go there and immerse myself in the culture, let me start from the top down." Snoop dug deep into reggae history and music (he is a musicologist at heart); he really zoned out and got into the vibe . . . and then came the request to get his hair locked. This was an intuitive dedication, perhaps some part spiritually and some part psychologically, to respectfully enter into the world of Jamaican music and culture.

One thing Snoop hit me with right before we left was, "Let's not go to Jamaica to just sit in the studio. I got a month, let me explore the country and learn from the people." Suroosh and Codine, one of Vice's co-producers (who's also Jamaican), were instrumental in identifying culturally significant locations for us to experience. In the spirit of authenticity, Snoop also wanted to touch base with Damian and the Marley family, as Damian, and Julian first went out on a major State-side tour with Snoop for Lollapalooza, and there's a close kindred spirit between Snoop and the Marleys for a long time.

SUROOSH: As we were exploring Jamaica together, some of the guys from your team, Snoop's day-to-day manager Kevin Barkey and his A&R Justin Li, kept saying, "things are going so well"—not that things don't go well on other projects, but there was a certain vibe going on the shoot when we were up at Strawberry Hill. There was something magical happening on a creative level while we were down there, and it was very pervasive in that it went through everything that we were doing. Even from a logistical perspective—if we had a shoot that was supposed to start at noon, and we were always running on

Jamaican time plus Snoop time, which means being three hours late, and I'm freaking out about the sun going down and losing our natural light from a shooting perspective—but every single day as the sun was going down as we were finishing our filming, I was like, "We got it. It's a wrap. We nailed it." It was almost like there was a larger force guiding us through this, and I think it affected everything we were doing, whether it was us making the movie or the producers making the album. Like we were saying in Jamaica, we were guided by Jah, and I really started to think that there was something to that. There was something else going on here, something very special about the project overall, which speaks to why we wanted to document it and put this book out as well, so we could capture it as almost a historical moment. When we met Willie T, who is a longtime personal photographer of Snoop's, we didn't know who he was, he was this kind of funny Guatemalan, but everyone calls him Mexican. Maybe ex-gangbanger, incredibly talented character and fantastic photographer, his favorite restaurant is Chipotle. And he was helping us out on our shoot when we needed a third camera, and he was just snapping away all day, and to be honest, I was like, "Whatever, just another random person on the shoot," but when I saw his photos for the first time when we sat down—I think we had some time off and he was just showing me some of the black-and-white shots he'd taken that day—and it hit me as to how talented he is.

And then, prior to leaving for Jamaica, we sent Snoop a big box of Vice swag before we went down with books and records and DVDs and magazines, so he could become more familiar with our output, and Snoop said, "Those books that you sent me, I loved them. I would love a book like that." And he said that right as I was thinking that we should do a coffee-table photo book of this trip, and so it was just one of these very natural/logical ideas. It was actually Snoop's suggestion. He said, "*I* want a book," to which I replied, "And I would be honored to make it."

Going back to this whole "magic vibe" thing that I was talking about earlier, I think it also has to do with gaining a deeper understanding of positivity from this trip and being in Jamaica. Growing up listening to reggae music, you always hear about "positive vibrations," and it's been commoditized, and you see it everywhere on T-shirts, and just kind of reggae-themed merchandise. But it wasn't until I was in Jamaica and immersed in the culture with all of you, with Snoop and Ted and my team, and we met with the Nyabinghi Rastafarians who were channeling this kind of positivity and love towards us, that something clicked. At that point I felt like I got a deeper understanding of what it means, what this "positive vibes" shit is all about. It elevated us.

TED: I think for Snoopadelic Films, Vice, and Stampede: we're always immersed and have an appreciation for all kinds of music and film—but you don't always get a chance to explore one particular genre in-depth. Some of us had a cursory understanding of reggae music and Rastafari culture, but I really got educated—I think we all did—on the origins of Rastafari, the social significance of the Rastas worldwide, and even the more spiritual and livity aspects of Rastafari—from the fundamentals of the Ital diet to the teachings of His Imperial Majesty Haile Selassie I. When at the Nyabinghi Temple, it was a blessing for the congregation to prepare a whole Ital meal and overstand the spiritual use of ganja . . . That whole experience was amazing. There's still a lot for me personally to learn about reggae music and Rastafari as a way of life, but the opportunity provided a whole depth of appreciation for Reggae artists and the historical significance of their songs.

The word "serendipity" has come up numerous times throughout the "Reincarnated" project, as it unfolded at a critical time in everyone's lives.

Vice was at the turning point of defining itself as a major media company globally for youth culture, and Snoop and Stampede were really on the forefront of how artists communicate and create content online, with Snoop being one of the most influential figures on social networks. There was just this place and time we were all at where the project had a significant impact. And while Snoop's fans are given the rare opportunity to participate in the effect of his Jamaican baptism, even the crew documenting the process and producing the project stepped away from the experience with a totally refreshed spirituality and philosophy. Suroosh started this moniker "PVC," Positive Vibes Crew, when we all returned to Babylon and had to go back to our day-to-day business—just to try to maintain that unique spirit that Jamaica gives you! The crew didn't know each other that well going in, but I think a lot of people walked away with close friends and lifelong relationships that only Jamaica could have provided.

SUROOSH: Absolutely. It's so rare to come out of a project and for it to have that kind of effect. We've been filming 7–8 years now, and this project more than others has created this bond. It had that effect on us and brought us all together and turned us into a family. That was the big challenge when returning home. How do you maintain those vibes? When you do a pilgrimage, whether it's a religious pilgrimage and you go to Mecca for Hajj—it's almost like that. You come back, and you want to maintain that feeling and that spiritual connection. It's hard when you're confronted with the challenges of day-to-day life and business, and I think that's why the PVC concept was a reminder even for myself, so you remember to keep things in perspective. It's like a self-help group (laughs). And ultimately this *Reincarnated* thing had a reincarnating effect on a lot of us while we were down there.

> "NEXT TIME I SEE YOU,
> WE'LL BE DOIN' IT. IT'S ON.
> I'LL SEE YOU IN JAMAICA."
> —SNOOP

TED: The last thing I would add is—in the same way that director Andy Capper developed a unique relationship with Snoop to hear stories that have never been shared with anyone else, there was a unique trust that developed between Snoop and Willie T, our book's photographer, to have rare access while we were in Jamaica, and to get these images you're about to see. Willie T captured truth: from capturing behind the scenes of the album's production to being right next to Snoop and Shante while they were experiencing elevation at the Nyabinghi Temple. Snoopadelic Films has produced a lot of content for Snoop's fans, and the accolades which *Reincarnated*'s film and photos have garnered speak to the depth of the project. From honors at the Toronto International Film Festival to SXSW, *Reincarnated* manifested as a true transmedia project, capturing Snoop's reggae journey inspired by positivity, unity, and struggle. It's a proud testament from the entire team to see how Snoop's courage to achieve balance and growth has influenced so many people around the world. Jah!

SUROOSH: Rastafari!

I.

DOGG DAYS

SNOOP SPEAKS

VICE GLOBAL EDITOR AND DIRECTOR OF *REINCARNATED* ANDY CAPPER SAT DOWN WITH SNOOP TO REFLECT ON HIS EXPERIENCE IN JAMAICA AND HIS CURRENT AND PAST INCARNATIONS.

VICE: During this trip we took you out of the comfort zone you're usually in when making a record.

SNOOP: A great rock and roller in heavy metal always jumps into the crowd to let the crowd feel him; I've always been a dive-in type of guy. Not jumping off the stage and into the crowd, per se, but more personally.

A young Snoop with keyboard and gun, acid-wash jeans, circa 1980s. The collages in this section were made by his high-school sweetheart and wife of twenty years, Shante Broadus.

VICE: When we went to Tivoli Gardens, a lot of people got up close and personal.

SNOOP: That was special with the little kids. A lot of them don't have TV, so when they do get a chance to see TV, they see me on the screen, then they see me in their neighborhood, and it's astonishment; it's love and respect. They know that I'm the same kind of person they are, the same rebel they are; I represent the same thing they represent, so they welcome me into their neighborhood. I'm not an outcast coming in, I'm a big brother or someone who represents the same spirit they do.

VICE: Walking onto the roof was kind of a nod to that first "Who Am I (What's My Name)?" video.

SNOOP: Yeah, walking onto the roof reminded me of that video on Long Beach. It was my first video in my neighborhood, and I had my whole community on the ground. They were watching me and supporting me and dancing to the music; they were looking up to me. It gave me a lot to aspire to, so, hopefully, it did a great thing for them.

VICE: How did you organize that video on Long Beach?

SNOOP: It was very unorganized. Y'all didn't see the behind the scenes, the fights, and the things that were rolled on that video day—and the day after. But, you know, by grace it happened. It was meant to be, and that is what it was. It turned out for the better. I want to give a shout-out to Fab 5 Freddy for putting together that video.

VICE: We visited Tivoli Gardens to see what it was like after the police had removed the infamous drug lord Dudus from the area. Situations like that happen all over the world, and it is a theme that runs through this movie, where the government pretends to be doing something good or right, but it actually doesn't benefit the poor.

SNOOP: The system is designed to break you down when you get to a certain point, no matter who you are, when you aren't controllable, when they feel you have too much power, when they feel that you're stronger than them. America has a great way of doing that, of going into other people's business and sniffing other people's shit and trying to fix other peoples' problems instead of fixing their own. They should let Jamaican justice deal with Dudus, let the people over there deal with him, they felt he wasn't that bad. Whatever he's being charged for in America . . . we've got bigger problems to worry about, like terrorism—as opposed to somebody who means so much to his community they call him the president.

VICE: When you grow up in a rough area like that, people misunderstand you. I remember one of my first exposures to you was the *Daily Star* article. [*When Snoop first visited Britain in 1994 to promote Doggystyle, he was on trial for murder. The UK Daily Star ran a full-blown, front-page picture of Snoop with the caption "Kick this evil bastard out!"*]

SNOOP: You know, [Tim] Westwood, the whole crew, whoever, wherever I went in London, it was all love. It was just the old people, Parliament, the mothafuckas from back in the '20s and '30s, with their old ways of thinking who thought that I was a murderer, even though I'd been acquitted. At that time, the queen gave me permission to come to town 'cause she had some grandbabies that liked Snoop Dogg—grandbabies who grew up to be princes. It felt good, like I'd made it, 'cause London was so far-fetched from where I come from. To be accepted in London meant that I was accepted, period. It was only the ones wearing the white wigs who wanted me out—not the people in the real world. They love me, 'cause every time I go, they give me love.

VICE: It is crazy to think that when you guys started, your lyrics freaked out a lot of people. Nowadays, they are nothing.
SNOOP: Those lyrics were our life, so I don't understand how they freaked people out. We lived it. It was a matter of us taking our lives and putting it on wax. There were movies out—*Menace II Society*, *Boyz n the Hood*, *Colors*—that depicted the same things that we were rapping about, so it wasn't a make-believe situation. I don't know why it scared people; it should have forewarned them that we were on a mission to do something right 'cause we recognized that there was a problem.

VICE: You're kind of fulfilling the role of a VICE journalist on this trip. When the West Coast movement started and the L.A. Riots happened, Chuck D from Public Enemy called artists like yourself, Ice Cube, and Dr. Dre "The Black CNN."
SNOOP: Yeah, I believe that we were, 'cause we were bringing the news uncut—and it was global. It wasn't restricted to California and the West Coast. We brought the news from everybody's perspective, and people respected us. We never aimed to make music for that reason. We did it 'cause we loved it, and it was something that we was going through. It was our expression at the time.

VICE: With this move into reggae, do you feel you're still making music and still telling stories to people?
SNOOP: I don't know. Reggae is a form of hip-hop, and hip-hop is a form of reggae. It's no different, and it's the same message. It's all about having fun and about peace, love, struggle, and happiness. I felt it was time for me to do something other than hip-hop, 'cause I've been on the top ever since I've been in it. I wanted to venture off into something else to see if I could conquer another genre and find myself while trying to conquer this music. I did that. I found who I was. I realized I'm somebody special and that I need to pay attention to the power I have and to focus on what I'm saying when people are listening.

VICE: And that prompted you to explore Rastafari?
SNOOP: I don't know why Rastafari called me. I believe you don't go searching for it; I believe it has to call you.

VICE: All the Rastas we know already knew that Snoop was a Rasta. How do you feel when they say that to you?
SNOOP: It felt like being welcomed by your family; like you had been lost at birth, grew up, became a man then found your family, all of them—your grandmomma, your uncles, your aunties, your little brothers, your little cousins. They're happy to see you and you're happy to see them, and they welcome you like they understand what you're going through, like, "We're going to help you find your way to where you need to be. Not where you are."

VICE: Were you aware of the significance of what they said at the

Rasta temple? When the empress baptized you she said, "The prodigal son has returned" and gave you the name "Berhane," which was Bob Marley's name. We found it shocking 'cause when we first talked about this project, you said, "I am Bob Marley reincarnated." When that happened, you probably thought that we staged it.
SNOOP: I still feel like y'all staged it.

VICE: That is the magic of this shoot, this project, and what you are doing.
SNOOP: That you mothafuckas staged everything, and it's working, you think so? [Laughs.] Y'all was there early. The Bob Marley T-shirts—you staged that—three nappie-headed kids over there with Bob Marley shirts on. Go over there, get over there, he's coming.

VICE: None of this has been staged at all. I didn't even research Berhane until we were at Tuff Gong, when I realized it was the same name. How did it feel? That whole trip to the Rasta temple? When you got there and it was dark?
SNOOP: It felt like when I got baptized in 1977, when I was a youngster at Trinity Baptist Church on 1401 East Gaviota Avenue, Long Beach, California. The Reverend Vynin, who I grew up with, took me and said, "Take me to the water," and the whole church started singing, and they baptized me, boom. I came out, and I was saved. I was replenished. I was clean. I was cleansed of all of my sins. It felt like that, but from a grown man's perspective. When I was young, I didn't understand why he was dunking my head in water, why there was singing, or what that meant. But as an old man, I understand the word *baptism*, and that I'd been baptized in the spirit that has always been in me but has always been trapped, 'cause I never knew how to allow it to come out. I wanted to let it out in bits and pieces, but I never could. I stood next to it, 'cause I didn't know what it was.

VICE: Can you describe the feeling you had when the empress laid her hands on you? 'Cause you were going to stand up to embrace her, and she was like, "Stand down."
SNOOP: That's the spirit, man. I watched a lot of TV, and I always looked at the great people from back in the day and the spirits of my ancestors. I know the elders, when they put their hands on you, it's for two reasons: either to bless you or to save you. And I felt like I was being saved, 'cause I'm already blessed. It was like she was saving me and keeping me on the path I need to be on. She was giving me the insight to lead the spirit within, to connect with their spirit, and to see that this is the only way to go.

VICE: The Rasta temple has kind of gone to you, "Here is the torch." How do you feel about that?
SNOOP: I love it. I love the responsibility. I love the challenge. I love being the advocate, the spokesperson. I love doing the right thing. I love making music that represents who Rastas are and what they stand for. That was my whole purpose. I didn't want to just come here and say I made a record in Jamaica, went to Bob Marley's studio, grew some dreadlocks, then went home. I wanted to get the experience, to become part of Rastafari.

VICE: What do you think Rastafari represents for someone who hasn't heard of it or doesn't know much about it?

SNOOP: Rastas represent peace, love, respect, intelligence, history, great guidance, the people you need in your life. With the craziness that is going on in the world, everybody's picking and choosing and putting religion, war—all kind of things—before you. These are the only people I've met who really stand for and mean peace. They live it and stomp down on it. It's their way of life, their culture.

VICE: What do you think of your violent days now? Do you ever have nightmares about them?
SNOOP: I never had nightmares, but I was always concerned with whether or not I was going to live to see another day, 'cause there was so much violence around, and you always had to be active. You couldn't just hide in the house or turn the other cheek; you had to be a part of it. You had to get in the mix. And where I stayed at was always in the mix. So I was either on tour with somebody or rolling with the wrong people. I became who I am 'cause I have a way with words. Being a little lyrical and rapping was beginning to become something special. I would make gangbang raps, and the homies would try to push me away from the gangbanging and into rhyming rhymes. That was my first call out of gangbanging and into rapping—and from rapping into what I'm doing now.

"I DON'T KNOW WHY RASTAFARI CALLED ME. I BELIEVE YOU DON'T GO SEARCHING FOR IT; I BELIEVE IT HAS TO CALL YOU."
—SNOOP

VICE: Was it your time in prison that made you see with clarity that you are a great rapper and that is what you wanted to do?
SNOOP: I think that time, one of my last times being locked away, I was this close to being with Dre, then I went to jail. I was in there rapping and everybody was like, "Yo, that shit is hard. You don't have to be in here." And that is when I knew I had to leave the homies alone, stop selling dope, stop hanging in the hood, and really fully get with Dre. I had to sleep on his floor, hustle and struggle, start off as nothing, to become something.

VICE: Was it hard to leave those old buddies behind?
SNOOP: It was really tough 'cause that world was all I knew, the habitat and environment I was used to being in. I could find something to eat, something to wear, somewhere to stay, females—everything was there for me and I could get it. In this world, I was a new baby, wet behind the ears. I didn't know how to write songs, how to take the lead, how to melodically do what I wanted to do. I had to grow into who I am. Dr. Dre allowed me to experiment and work with this artist named the D.O.C., who gave me the formula. And when he gave me the formula, I became Snoop Doggy Dog.

VICE: The Alpha Boys school was special, did you have anything like that when you were a kid? [a "residential child-care institution in Kingston Jamaica, owned and operated by the Sisters of Mercy, a Catholic order of Nuns committed to working with the poor, sick, and uneducated"

according to their website. It has a very famous music program credited with giving birth to the musical sensibilities of some of reggae's forefathers and, thus, reggae itself. They also very explicitly see music and education as a combatant to violence.]
SNOOP: Not that I knew of.

VICE: I read in your book that there was an exchange program and that you would go to a white part of town, stay with them, and play Xbox.
SNOOP: When I was in junior high, I went to a school called Marshall Middle School in Lakewood, California. It was in a white neighborhood, so after school, I would hang with the white kids. I got in real cool with them, and it was cool with me. My mother taught me to love people, so I didn't have eyesight for colors. I became friends with a lot of kids who lived in the neighborhood, and they would bring me to their houses. Being the nigga that I was, I would steal and take shit and do the kind of shit that niggas do. It's what it was. I didn't mean any harm by it but, you know, you shouldn't have me in your mothafuckin' house.

VICE: The Alpha Boys program is a different thing. This is encouraging kids, teaching them an instrument. . .
SNOOP: Nah, this program is special 'cause it teaches sports, music, and mentality—one if not all three are a necessity in everything that goes on in the world. So to be taught that and instilled with the right direction is key 'cause school doesn't always teach you what you need to know when you are out of school, it only teaches you the shit you need when you're in school and that is bad sometimes 'cause a lot of dudes get out of school and that shit that they've been taught doesn't work. This why so many people with college degrees don't have jobs right now, 'cause that shit they learned in school doesn't work. It's common sense that gets you by in the real world. To have street knowledge and book knowledge is awesome, but you need a fine medium to do what you really want. To really succeed, you need to have both.

VICE: You've talked about your mom's influence on you growing up as well.
SNOOP: Man, my momma had old-school Southern values and would whoop my ass if I fucked up. I was scared of her. I respected her and was scared of her at the same time so I didn't get too out-of-pocket and do, like, crazy shit like some of my other homies, who were going to jail for eighteen months, two to three years. I was getting like two months, ninety days, four months, eight months 'cause of the crimes that I was doing. When I was a juvenile, I always knew that I'd have to deal with my momma. She had strict rules in our house, and she had an iron fist, which was no issue, I was just lacking that father support, which made me drift off, and hang out with gangs and certain homies, drug dealers doing shit that was influential to my eyes. I had no male guidance and my mother couldn't teach me how to be a man. She could only be my mother.

VICE: You also talk about when you were no longer a juvenile, you were an adult, and your mom didn't come to see you in prison.
SNOOP: She didn't come see me when I was locked up in prison; I don't know why, but I feel like it was tough love. I was fucked up. I understand her and respect what she did. At the time, I was mad and discouraged. I was feeling like she didn't love me and had left me for dead, but at the

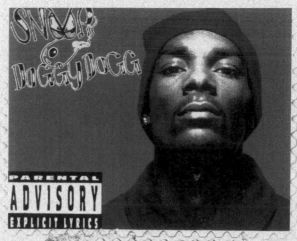

RAPPER

Tha Doggfather

PRAYERS

ANSWERED

ACTOR

same time, the values that she instilled in me should have prevented me from going there. It was the decisions and choices I made that got me there, so I had to suck it up and man up and say to myself that if I ever have kids and am put in that position, I may have to do the same thing. I may have to ignore my son or daughter for them to understand the love I'm giving, 'cause sometimes, as kids, we expect the love as opposed to appreciating it. Sometimes it goes unappreciated 'cause you expect it so much.

VICE: The female role model thing . . . there's the lady who baptized you, but there is also the story of Nanny of the Maroons, the runaway slave.
SNOOP: It was special, man. I can't imagine people having to, like, walk to get to that destination. I ain't ever driven so far as I have on this mothafuckin' trip. I'm gonna throw up the next time I get in the car. We've got to get a boat or something, a helicopter, I'll even parasail to the next location. If I was white, my whole face would be pink right now. It was tucked away. It was far, it was secure, it was what it needed to be to understand Nanny and what she stood for and what she had to do. As we took that journey, it was like going to the Promised Land. It's a long way, but when you get there, it's happiness. You see the lights and her grave site; you see the river and the story of the spirits. To me, Nanny is like Jamaica's Harriet Tubman, 'cause she freed the slaves. She stood up with the vengeance of a male. She had brothers and other family members who helped her, but she took charge and had a real plan. She had a military mind and moved with swiftness—in a sort of supernatural way, is what they say—that was effective.

VICE: Did the sound of the drums of the Maroons inform the record at all?
SNOOP: The songs that the Maroons were singing are more than a hundred years old. It made me want to make music that's still here fifty or sixty years from now, connect people with my spirit even after I'm gone.

VICE: How did your wife find the Maroons and the rest of the temple?
SNOOP: She had a great experience. I think it was a baptism for her as well. She needed that to know that I was in the mood for change 'cause I'm reckless at times. She sees it more than anybody. I really wanted her to be here to be a part of what I'm doing, as opposed to my past records, which have always been me rolling to the studio and her not being connected to the records. This record is peace, love, struggle, happiness—everything I'm going through.

VICE: You were high school sweethearts [her collages are in these pages].
SNOOP: Well, I mean, I was out of high school when she was in high school, but I used to hang around the high school, you know what I'm saying?

VICE: How long have you been together?
SNOOP: About twenty years.

VICE: What's the secret to a long-lasting marriage? I really want to know.

SNOOP: What's the secret? You gotta be willing to sacrifice. You gotta be willing to put what matters first. In the beginning I loved her a lot, way more than she loved me, before she was my woman. When I became successful, it went the other way around. Then we went through a stage where it was a little bit of love; but the kids had our love, and it just boiled down to the fact that if this is really what you want, if this is who you say you really want to be with, then you got to make sacrifices to really love that person and make that person be a part of what you do. It's been a struggle, but at the same time, it's been healthy, it's been good, and it's been what it's supposed to be. This project has helped my home and my life in general, so I'm thankful for the move.

VICE: At the temple, at one point I looked over at you and Shante. You were together, and it was like all the cameras were gone and we weren't there. It was just you and your wife, and this group of people. She was just beaming. She looked so happy.
SNOOP: That's what she loves, and I've been always avoiding it, 'cause I'm a player. I've been trying to, you know, play and whatnot, but this was healthy, like I said, 'cause it's about change. It's about becoming a man and putting the right things in perspective and moving forward with the right movement and the right people. That's my backbone, and it's official.

VICE: Why now? Why is this kind of project happening right now? What was it inside of you that prompted the decision to pull the trigger on *Reincarnated*?
SNOOP: I don't know. I think just because it's so much death. There's so much death, there's so much destruction, there's so much mayhem, and there's so much misunderstanding in music. We're losing so many great musicians, and we don't love 'em while they're here. I want to be loved while I'm here, and the only way to get love is to give love. That's mainly why I believe that now is the time, 'cause there's really not a lot of love until you die. Nobody loves you while you're here. Nobody appreciates you, upholds you with greatness, until you're gone. I want that spirit while I'm here.

VICE: Was that anything to do with Nate Dogg's death?
SNOOP: It did have a lot to do with Nate Dogg, but not directly. It wasn't like after he died, I decided to seek and find it. It was over a period of time, with that being the main backdrop. That and other life experiences, and seeing other people leave here, and just my life in general, and looking at my family and where I want to be, and how I've got to prepare myself in order to be here.

VICE: I don't want to pry, but how did you deal with the Nate thing?
SNOOP: Man, that was real hard 'cause he was somebody that I started with, and when I say started with, I don't mean just musically. I mean, like, became a man with. I met Nate when I was in high school, in the tenth grade, and we just hooked up. We became friends from a science class, from PE and singing together, from me going to his house and him coming to my house. It was deep, man. It was like losing my brother, and I ain't ever really going to get over that. I try to be strong and keep everybody around me strong 'cause they look at me like the head of it all. If I'm weak, then everybody else is gonna be weak. But there were certain moments when I couldn't do anything but be weak. A piece of me was

gone, and they understood that. We all got back strong, and we're back on our feet. We're doing what we're supposed to be doing, but I believe we all understand our journey better now. We understand that we have a mission to accomplish. No more playing games. No more disrespecting your body and not thinking and being reckless.

VICE: That gang of brothers you talk about, I guess that's Warren G—
SNOOP: Warren G, Kurupt, Nate Dogg, Daz—they're like my blood brothers. We started out drinking from the same forties, sleeping on the same floors, sharing the same blankets, wearing the same clothes, eating out of the same chicken box, smoking out of the same twenty bag. Blood brothers. But at the same time, you grow old, get families, responsibilities, and you get things in life that take you away from your extended family, 'cause you have an immediate family. I believe that's where we are right now, even though I try my best to keep all of us together, for the most part, this project right here is me spreading my wings and becoming my own bird, flying away. I built a lot of nests, but it's time for all the birdies to fly on their own, let the eagles soar.

VICE: It's not the first time you've gone off by yourself, right?
SNOOP: When I left Death Row to join No Limit? Yep, that was the first time I did it. I had to protect myself. I had to spread my wings. I had to look out for me and my family and do what was best. It was dangerous, 'cause I was up against the enemy, and when the enemy's coming after you, he's going to use any and all means necessary. It prepared me for my future and who I am now; it built me into the player that I am now, the person that I am now, and the man that I am now. It shaped and molded me to become strong and mentally sharp, so I'm grateful for those moments and to be able to take off and transform and find new life. I feel that right now is the best time for me to do this 'cause I'm in a great space, and I'm ready to fly.

VICE: When you think of those Death Row days with 2Pac and everything, how does that make you feel?
SNOOP: Oh, the Death Row days . . . I'm not one of those bitter people, so it doesn't make me feel bad. I remember the great times on Death Row. We were the baddest mothafuckas in the world. Our music was the shit. Everybody loved us; we had Mexicans, Blacks, Bloods, and Crips all on the same page, and that was the first time ever we had everybody agreeing 'cause of the music that we made. It was peace treaty time. It was love, it was happiness. We had money, and we were able to give our friends and family jobs and create opportunities. I had a record label. I was putting out artists, doing videos. I did my first movie, *Murder Was the Case*. I got the idea for it from Michael Jackson's *Thriller*. I told Suge I wanted to do an eighteen-minute movie. He believed in me, and we did it. We made it a soundtrack—I told them I wanted to put Daz and Kurupt and Tha Dogg Pound on it. They did it, and it went double platinum.

All the shit I wanted to do, they allowed me to do. I had fun. I told Suge to get 2Pac out of the penitentiary and put him on Death Row with us. I gave him songs to make his record sound dope, rapped on songs with him, hung out with him, brought him to my house, let him become a part of my family, and see the shit that I had, let him get influenced by that. Then he brought me to his world and influenced me with Hugo Boss suits, Italian jewelry, and shit that I could never even explain or pronounce. He turned me on to things that made me a bigger, brighter person, so it was a give-take relationship; and it was a love–hate relationship 'cause we loved what we did, but we hated the fact that it didn't last forever.

VICE: It's one of the greatest rock-and-roll stories, I think.
SNOOP: I think so, too. We don't talk about it a lot 'cause it's a lot of bad blood and negativity. But if people just looked at the good times and the success of the records and the things that we did . . . I did the *American Music Awards*, I did *Soul Train*, I did everything.

Dick Clark fought for me to be on ABC. When they were like, "Fuck that, he can't be on ABC," Dick Clark was like, "I've been doing the *American Music Awards* for thirty fucking years; this nigga's coming on, and he's doing his shit." I had a 'fro in my shit, I had a natural picked out. I came out and did my shit, and Dick Clark came out and gave me a hug. I was like, "Man, Dick Clark knows who the fuck I am." And from that day on, Dick was always my homie till the last time I saw him. Shout–out to Dick Clark. He's a real mothafucka, you know what I'm saying?

"I BUILT A LOT OF NESTS, BUT IT'S TIME FOR ALL THE BIRDIES TO FLY ON THEIR OWN, LET THE EAGLES SOAR."

—SNOOP

VICE: It seems like the whole Death Row thing was an important part of your journey, and I think *The Chronic* made you a better businessman and made you understand that you needed to be Snoop Dogg the rapper and do *Doggystyle*.
SNOOP: *The Chronic* was my internship. I've hired more than a hundred interns. They've become big, bright business mothafuckas. I listened to that record about three days ago, and it's, like, I wrote about twelve songs on that mothafuckin' album, like really wrote—from top to bottom, the verse and the hook, Dre's part, Daz's part, my part—and I'm looking at that shit, like, the money doesn't even matter; it's the training I got in how to make records, to put together rhythms and melodies and inserts and skits and my voice. Dre let me do what the fuck I wanted to do back then. It wasn't like, "No, tell me what to do." He basically depended on me. It was like being able to throw all of this paint on the board so Dr. Dre could create a picture. But that paint created my picture.

On a couple of projects, I became more of a business. I did shows. I went out and created my name. I could always get money and do shit, whether Dre wanted to or not. I don't even know why I did it—'cause I was always thinking it was going to be me and him. But the way I set it up, I can stand on my own feet to this day, but when he's ready to roll, we're gonna hit that road together. In a good way—I wouldn't want anybody else to get his back but me 'cause I'm like Robin and he's Batman when it comes to that duo shit. That is the position I feel that I'm in 'cause of the moves I've made, like if he goes on tour, he has to take me, as opposed to when I go on tour, I can go by myself—with or without him. It would be nice if I had A, B, and C, but at the same time, people are paying to see D, O, double G.

VICE: What does Dre think of your trip to Jamaica? *[This interview took place during the making of* Reincarnated, *before the album and documentary were released.]*
SNOOP: He doesn't know about it. Nobody knows about it. I haven't really released this information to anybody. I'm just broadcasting, telling people what I'm doing 'cause it's a movement, an experience—and it's hard to explain an experience and a transformation. People have to just see it and witness it 'cause it's too hard to just sit them down and tell them, "This is this, and this is this." I've told only a few people, the chosen few, 'cause I want certain elements of music and certain elements of hearsay floating around. But people like Dr. Dre, who is critical of my music, I don't want him to see it, touch it, or hear it until it's fine-tuned. Then he can be astonished by it.

VICE: How about Daz, was he one of the chosen few?
SNOOP: Yeah, he's my little cousin, he comes with everything. When I wrote "Murder Was the Case," which is one of the strongest songs I ever wrote, it started as a song called "Dave" and Daz was sittin' next to me. He's like, "You should do a deal with the devil and sell your soul to the devil." And I'm like, "Aight . . . Bring your lifestyle to me I'll make it better / And how long will I live? / Eternal life and forever / And will I be, the G that I was? / I'll make your life better than you can imagine or even dreamed of / So relax your soul, let me take control / Close your eyes, my son / My eyes are closed." When he came up with that piece, right there, it set off "Murder Was the Case"—"'Cause now I know where I'm going. I'm fresh out my coma / I got my momma and my daddy and my homies and my corner / It's gonna take a miracle they say / For me to walk again and talk again in any way. . ." So now I'm on a journey and my little cousin is telling me where to go next. When I get to the third verse, my other cousin Joe Cool says, "Now go to 'Chino, rollin' on the gray goose," but Daz said do the prayer first. "Now I lay me down to sleep," so you understand what I'm saying, it was like these are people I trust, who understand my struggle. He maybe couldn't have written that for me, but he could get me going in the direction necessary to make my pen go down that lane to write that kind of material. By him being here, he created "Ashtrays and Heartbreaks," and that is my favorite song 'cause it just means the most. If he hadn't been here that song would have never happened.

VICE: How has he been finding Jamaica and the Rasta stuff?
SNOOP: Daz is a playboy. He likes to play a lot and he plays like a boy. He's always going to be my little cousin, I'll always envision him that way.

VICE: The other night at Ali's birthday celebration, you said he wasn't a father figure for all the kids in the building.
SNOOP: I meant that Muhammad Ali was not a father figure in the neighborhood 'cause he was our *father*. To be a father *figure* is to be someone who gets it right; to be a father is to be someone whose struggle and pain you see and come to understand, and that is somebody you want to be like. You really want to be like your father. You want to walk in his shoes. You want to impress him. When you made it you always looked to see if Muhammad Ali knew who you were 'cause once you were crowned by the champ, you'd made it.

VICE: He was very much an antiestablishment figure, too.
SNOOP: He was. He went through the hard times, the bad times. He had a lot on his shoulders that he had to deal with to become the greatest of all time—not just in the ring but out of it, too. Standing up, being about something, that meant a lot, especially to our culture 'cause nobody was standing up. Everybody was turning the other cheek, and nobody was being, as they say, militant or defensive or offensive. I loved him for that. That is why I cherished the moment onscreen with him. I can always look at that and say that I knew Muhammad Ali and Muhammad Ali knew me. He's not just a human spirit, he's a spirit that's gonna live on. That's why so many people love him, and for me to connect to him lets me know that I'm going to live on.

VICE: Back to the album for a second, are you going to rap on the record? That is what everyone is talking about in the studio.
SNOOP: I want to do an entire record with no rappin' 'cause that will show my growth as an artist, to be able to restrain myself and not rap. I got rap songs that will never die, that I'm gonna do until I'm sixty years old, and what else could I do in the rap world that is appealing like that? As for me staying true to the culture of this music, and doing what this music was made to do, and sing on it . . . I can sing. Hell, yeah.

VICE: Who is it in the studio that most wants you to rap?
SNOOP: Probably the writers. I don't think it's Diplo and the producers. They don't really care. They don't give a fuck. A song is a song to them. But the writers who are writing this material? They are Snoop Dogg fans, so they like the shit that I do as a rapper. It's like, "Come on, nigga, you got to do at least one. I could hear you busting on that one." I'm like, "Yeah, it's like an R&B single, right?" And if the R&B single decides to go rap, they're going to tell that R&B singer, "Man, would you please sing one hook." "Nah, I'm rapping now." You gotta stick to the script. I know mothafuckas don't think I'm going to do a good job at it, but at the same time, I'm going to do a great job at it.

VICE: We are all listening to the songs thinking this is going to be huge.
SNOOP: It's going to be gigantic. I've never had songs like these. These songs are songs that could get played on any radio station, and I've always had songs that are limited that way. If I did have a pop song, it was sexual, it was weed related, it was crime related. So it was something that was too much. I remember I did "Sexual Eruption," and that was a really big crossover song for me, but some radio stations were like, "Change the name to 'Sensual Seduction.'" Fuck change the name. Sing the words like this, OK. Fuck it. So like these songs, I don't have to change shit. Just, bam, 'cause they're songs of unity and love and peace, and everybody needs that right now. That's going to fit on every radio station. I got shit that is going to fit on every radio station.

DAZ

★ **AS WELL AS BEING SNOOP'S COUSIN, DAZ IS A LEGEND OF WEST COAST HIP-HOP, HAVING PERFORMED ON AND PRODUCED RECORD-BREAKING HITS FOR 2PAC, DR. DRE, SNOOP, AND HIS OWN GROUP, THA DOGG POUND. HE JOINED SNOOP ON HIS JOURNEY TO JAMAICA AND THIS IS WHAT HE HAD TO SAY ABOUT IT.**

VICE: How old were you when you first met Snoop?
DAZ: We're cousins, probably eight months or one year old. We grew up together—takin' baths together, getting our asses whooped together—everything, from day one. And everything's got to do with music in our family—my mom wrote songs for the Bobby "Blue" Band, our uncles were in a group called the Sensational Varnado Brothers. They were the ones that gave Snoop the roach when he was seven and introduced him to Bob Marley's music. Then Snoop and I made our own group Tha Dogg Pound in 1992.

VICE: What was it like growing up with Snoop? Any interesting stories?
DAZ: We used to hang out at Michael Jackson's house. My mom was a schoolteacher, she tutored Janet Jackson, and

she knew a lot of people 'cause she wrote songs for 'em, produced for 'em, and we were hangin' out there and everything. It was real cool when we were young; me and Snoop, we did a lot. We still doin' a lot.

VICE: How was Michael Jackson's house?
DAZ: You know, it was in that time of "Thriller," around that time of *Off the Wall*. He had the afro.

VICE: You and Snoop with Michael Jackson? With an afro?
DAZ: Yeah, I've gotta find the pictures. My mom's got them.

VICE: What was the idea behind Tha Dogg Pound?
DAZ: You know, just strugglin', survivin', and tryin' to make good music. Before that, I was just producing with Dr. Dre. We started putting our music together and, you know, once you put a lot of music together, it starts shining. So the word was out; the buzz was out and there was a demand for us. When nobody else produced for us, I learned how to produce and put it together. And when you learn that, you just step up and pass everybody. That's what we did.

"EVERYTHING'S GOT TO DO WITH MUSIC IN OUR FAMILY."
—DAZ

VICE: And that was the attitude of Tha Dogg Pound. For me, there's that video *What Would You Do*. What's the attitude in that video?
DAZ: We shot *two* videos. The first one we shot was, like, with a bunch of other people. Then we did another one with Dr. Dre. We were just learnin' what the cameras are and learnin' this and that. I'm an observer. I just watch and observe, tricklin' in my brain, and try to do it myself.

VICE: After that period you went on to produce for whom?
DAZ: I started producin' for Dr. Dre. I did *The Chronic*. After that I went to *Doggystyle*, then *Dogg Food*, then I started producin' 2Pac.

VICE: Which 2Pac records did you make?
DAZ: I did the first album—*All Eyez on Me*. I did "2 of Amerikaz Most Wanted," "Ambitionz az a Ridah," "I Ain't Mad at Cha," "Skandalouz," and "Got My Mind Made Up." The first five songs on the album. Wow. Yep.

VICE: How were those days? Being in that scene? You hear mythical stories about it.
DAZ: Yeah, I miss those days. When I smell the air, it reminds me of different little things. Lookin' back at what we've been through, what we surpassed and overcame in twenty years; it's still relevant. It's a blessing, to keep on hearing it and doing it, even though we're still makin' history *now*.

VICE: Yeah, you are. So how'd you feel about the party last night?
[*During the shoot in Jamaica, Snoop and Daz went to Las Vegas for twenty-four hours so Snoop could perform at Muhammad Ali's seventieth birthday.*]
DAZ: Last night was a celebration, and it was celebrity. It was real shit. All the celebrity A+ were there: Muhammad Ali, every boxer you know except Joe Frazier, every celebrity from Ne-Yo, Puffy–Stevie Wonder flew in from Whitney Houston's funeral. We were in the back, kickin' with Quincy Jones. It was *star-studded*. We got Joe Perry from Aerosmith. We got a little bit of everybody on tape. It's just a segment of a day *off* from what we are doin,' to let you know how we be movin' and groovin' through the world.

VICE: How was Puffy?
DAZ: Puffy acted regular, like Puffy acts. But when that dude with the tequila showed up, it was all business. He turned into a vigilante. Nobody even knew what the guy who *made* Patrón looked like. Now we got him on tape.

VICE: Who was that?
DAZ: Guy named John Paul DeJoria. He was feelin' good, too. You know you always gotta test your own product [*laughs*].

VICE: What about "don't get high on your own supply"?
DAZ: Yeah, don't get *drunk* on your own supply! He had a big, humongous bottle. He said he started Patrón with $500 of his own money. He bought out some kids who were makin' bootleg Patrón. You can't beat that. Now he's five hundred billion dollars richer! He says he doesn't even see half the money–it just goes to charities and stuff like that. If he does a deal with you, he wants you to give fifty percent to charity, you know, to help the world, or whatever cause.

VICE: That's great. You said before that when you walked up to Ali, he didn't seem to recognize you.
DAZ: Yeah, he was looking like, "Who is this mothafucka talking to me?" But then with Snoop, he just turned into a whole 'nother person. So it was, like, real genuine. Got it all on tape for you. We also talked to several people who are down to do something on the album.

VICE: Yes, how do you feel the record's going? You only heard it recently, right? Do you work with Snoop closely?
DAZ: Yeah, he's my first cousin. I advise him, he advises me; we listen and put it together. But you know the music is coming out real slow and fast with Diplo. It's all the chemistry. Now that we're back with that power, it's gonna be a whole 'nother vibe [*laughs*]. We were stressed out at first, but now we're not. Everybody's gonna be smilin' around here.

VICE: This is maybe a bit personal, but do you think that Nate Dogg's death had anything to do with Snoop Dogg's decision to take this different path?
DAZ: Uh, no. There just comes a time in your life when you've gotta make a change, when you're sick and tired of doing the same thing. Everything repeats itself and you gotta try something different to be different, to get your mood swings changed. It's life; everyone changes. If you don't change, something's wrong with you.

VICE: Overall, the general experience of being here and all the Rasta stuff that you've been exposed to, how have you felt about that? I've seen you on the camera; you just look kind of like . . .

DAZ: I'm watchin', observin', takin' it all in, learnin'. When you want to learn something, you shut the fuck up and you listen. The fast people just be talking and shit, and I just listen and take everything that I heard and apply it to myself. 'Cause out here, it's really more like, about yourself, your spiritual self, and just learning. Out here you can only think to yourself, hear the birds. The only thing you might do is hear yourself go [*puff*].

"OUT HERE, IT'S REALLY MORE ABOUT YOURSELF, YOUR SPIRITUAL SELF, AND JUST LEARNING."

—DAZ

VICE: What do you think about the weed that Rastas carry compared to kush?

DAZ: It's grown organically, in the ground. What we get is grown in the house, so it's like two different things, but it's all good. Here, it's coming from the earth. It just comes to share the light. There's two different types of weed, there's sativa and there's indica. If you know what sativa is, and if you know what indica is, then you know what the difference is. They say indica is Lou Ferrigno and that sativa is like a featherweight. Two different powers. When I was at Tuff Gong studios I look up at the vents, and I'm like, "How much weed have they smoked in the vents?!" Cause, you know, you can see all the brown stuff and you know it's authentic. They left everything like it was. We wanted to add our smoke to the vents, so we just started blowin'.

II.

JAMAICA VISIONS

On the first day of shooting in February 2012, we visited a secret marijuana farm hidden deep in the Blue Mountains. It took an hour to drive there, followed by an hour-long hike through steep, winding jungle paths. When we got there, accompanied by a gang of friendly, machete-wielding Rastas, we met the girl pictured here on a mountaintop. She told us that she thought she recognized Snoop and gave him a fistful of handpicked flowers. Snoop and the Rastas sat on

top of the mountain and smoked weed they had grown, from huge chalices for hours. The amount of weed smoked combined with the altitude of the mountain range arguably made them, at that moment in time, the highest people on the planet.

"THE WEED HERE IS ORGANIC,
    STRAIGHT OUT THE GROUND, AND
IF YOU FIND A GOOD BUD,
    IT WILL GET YOU HIGH AS FUCK!"
                —SNOOP

The *Reincarnated* team of security, shooters, and producers after five hours climbing mountains and smoking acres of weed. Some of us at least. Included here are Suroosh Alvi (Producer), Andy Capper (Director), Justin Li (Co-Producer), William Fairman and Nick Neofitidis (Directors of Photography), Codine Williams (Co-Producer), Ted Chung (Producer), Dave Dale from the Blue Mountain Coffee House Boys, Paul "Prendy" Prendergast (Security), Keys (Security) (Artiste), and Jimmy Smith (Security). Oaz

39

KINGSTON STREET PARTY

A few days later, during our first night of recording at Tuff Gong, there was a dancehall party outside on the street. It was so loud, we could even hear it in the (allegedly) sound-proof studio. These parties happen on a daily basis around the country and especially in Kingston, where people just hang out on the streets. Often local DJs and entertainers show up, either to be with fans or release new tracks.

41

There are always groups who dance for the crowd and people are well familiar with being photographed in their fantastic and colorful outfits. There was even a guy in a wheelchair, who did not let that deter him from dressing up and gettin' down (pictured, mid-left).

45

★ Tivoli Gardens is one of Kingston's most legendary ghettos. We went there to see how it compared to Long Beach, where Snoop grew up. Tivoli Gardens was once the stronghold of the drug lord Christopher "Dudus" Coke. Along with dealing vast amounts of cocaine and marijuana, Dudus was a community leader of sorts and would provide money to the needy in the neighborhood. His gang, the Shower Posse, was said to have also self–policed the area. Dudus was extradited to the U.S. on allegations of drug trafficking, which created a kind of civil war on the island in May 2010 between his supporters and the Jamaican authorities, a situation which remains unresolved to this day. During our visit, many residents expressed that the community missed

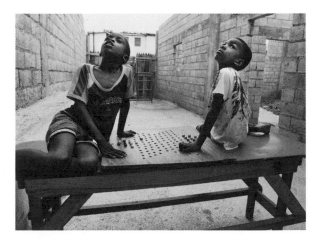

its former leader. Because Snoop grew up in a community partially run by Crip gangs, he felt an instant connection with the locals, who are experiencing cultural issues similar to his own.

"FROM THE DEPTHS
OF THE SEA / BACK TO
THE BLOCK . . ."

—SNOOP DOGG,
"WHAT'S MY NAME?"

While we were in Tivoli, people started audibly whispering that Snoop was in the neighborhood and gathered around to get a glimpse of him. The kids were especially excited. Even the police, who have been a constant presence in the neighborhood since Dudus's arrest, came out to see Snoop and pose for pictures.

February 18, 2012: Snoop had a recording session in a makeshift studio with local musician Cutty Corn and other DJs from Tivoli. It was super hot and sticky in the room, but they were having so much fun, they stayed locked in there for more than an hour, never noticing the crazy heat. It reminded Snoop of his early days in Long Beach, recording in VIP records, where he started his career with Nate Dogg, Warren G, and crew.

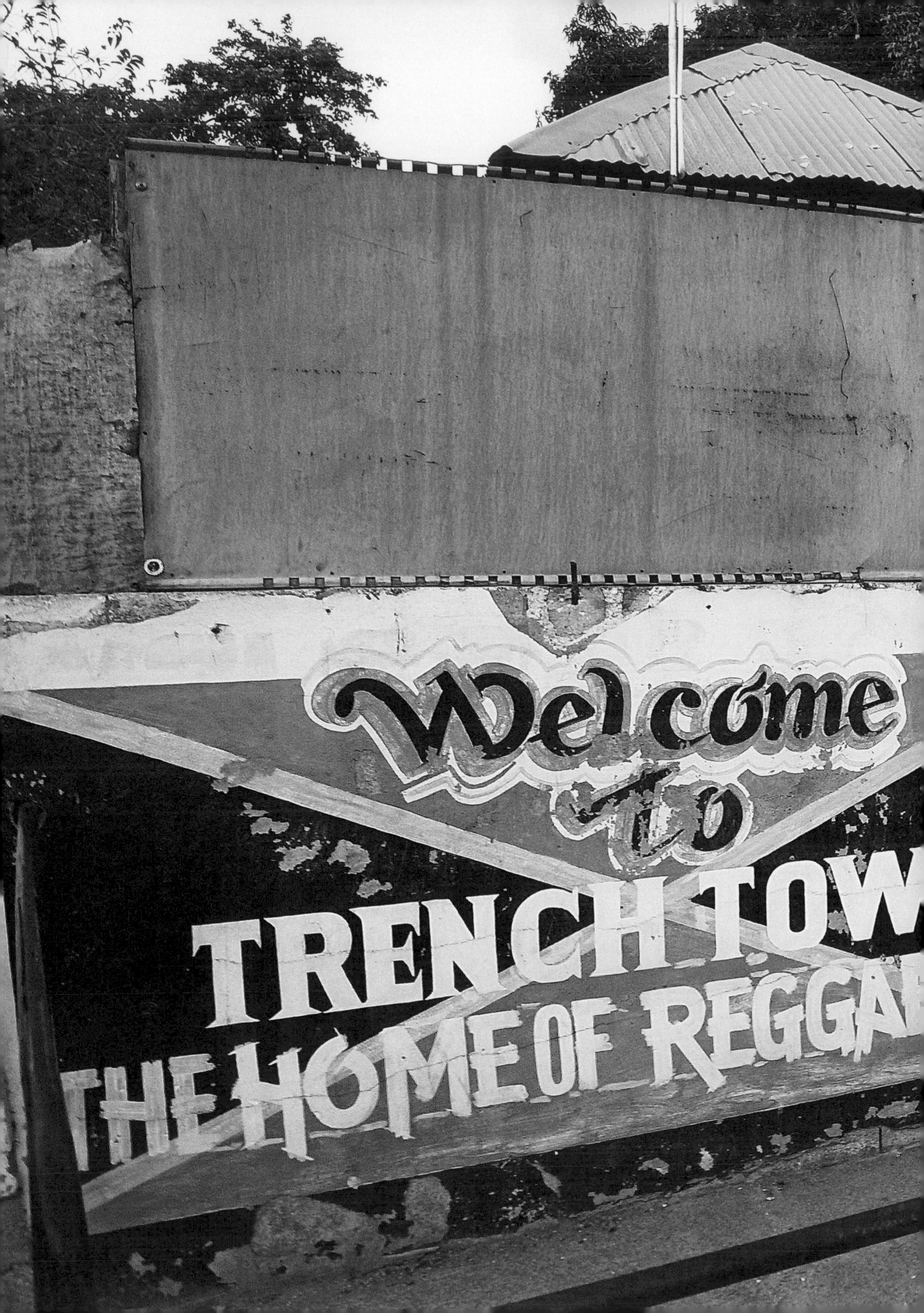
Welcome
to
TRENCH TOW
THE HOME OF REGGA

★ Bob Marley's home on Hope Road (in uptown Kingston), where he lived just before the attempt on his life, is now a small museum. In 1976, Bob tried to foster peace between rival political parties who were warring in the streets of Kingston during what was an election year. There was a brutal attempt on his life when assailants rained bullets on his entire home (which Bob had come to consider his safe "neutral" zone) using automatic weapons. It happened just days before he was to play a peace/love concert called Smile Jamaica. Damian "Junior Gong" Marley was also in attendance, and is, in many ways, charismatic and musically talented like his father. Only two when his father died and a three-time Grammy Award

winner, Damian has carried on his father's musical, as well as political legacy. His songs often center on propagating love and peace and awareness of Rastafari values.

TUFF GONG STUDIO

DAY 1 SNOOP PLAYLIST
~~-① -REWRITE!!

1. Dre -Runaway √√ Say what u wanna Say!√√
2. Dre - Say what u wanna Say! bridge/buk
3. Diplo - "BLVD" - Jah dan samplish √√√
4. ARTIBELLA - LAZER3 - √√√
5. CASH MACHINE - NOT √√√√
6. SUNDAY SONG - ? KIDS
7. HARDER TIMES - HAND P___SSION
8. NEVER GIVEUP - PROD. NEED __ORK - GT
9. IT RAINS
10. SOLONG - KEEPER!! LOVES IT! HA!
11. THINGS CHANGE - ROLLER SKATES- SCELE
12. REBURIEL →

BEAUTIFUL SONG
SNOOP 2 SING
PULSE

★ Bob Marley built Tuff Gong in 1965. The studio is so named because you had to be "Tuff" to survive in the music business in Jamaica. It was used to record all of Bob's albums, starting with *The Wailing Wailers*. Many recording artists make Tuff Gong a central destination in Jamaica to invoke the spirit of Bob in their music.

The *Reincarnated* recording sessions took place at Tuff Gong and Geejam in the last few weeks of February. Diplo gathered his team of writers and producers at the studio, including Angela Hunte-Wisner, Ariel Rechtshaid, Dre Skull, Andrew "Moon" Bain, and Jahdan Blakkamoore.

Every day, filming ended well past dark. The crew would pack up all the equipment then head to Tuff Gong to record the album until the early hours of the morning, only to begin filming again a few hours later. Snoop is pictured here taking a rare break while the crew works on mixes in the booth.

RITA MARLEY

★ Rita Marley was also visiting Jamaica and attended a "reasoning"–a Rastafarian meeting session with chants, prayers, singing, and community discussions–organized by her granddaughter. Rita graciously allowed the crew and Snoop to attend the event with her and dig further into Marley family history. She was there on the night of the attempt on Bob Marley's life in 1976 and barely survived.

While at the Marley Museum, Snoop took pictures of himself with Bob Marley's statue. He was approached by several people in the crowd and by a Rasta who started wearing with Haile Selassie I's face carved into it.

MARCUS GARVEY

A PEOPLE WITHOUT THE KNOWLEDGE OF THEIR PAST HISTORY, ORIGIN AND CULTURE IS LIKE A TREE WITHOUT ROOTS.

I KNOW NO NATIONAL BOUNDARY WHERE THE NEGRO IS CONCERNED. THE WHOLE WORLD IS MY PROVINCE UNTIL AFRICA IS FREE.

BUNNY
WAILER

SNOOP MET THE LEGENDARY NEVILLE "BUNNY WAILER" LIVINGSTON AT HIS COMPOUND IN THE HILLS OF KINGSTON FOR A CHILL SESSION IN FEBRUARY 2012. ALSO AT THE MEETING WERE PRODUCERS DIPLO AND DRE SKULL, AS WELL AS SNOOP AND BUNNY'S RESPECTIVE MANAGERS: TED CHUNG AND MAXINE STOWE.

BUNNY WAILER: Peter Tosh sang, "I want to be here to sing, the Wailers before us sang " . . . *that* is what we are protecting in this fifty-year anniversary of reggae music that is now right on our steps. I am always interested in exhibiting what comes from Bunny Wailer, to put another mark on reggae music. If Snoop comes to do that, then I would be in support of doing that with him and making reggae music more established. Snoop is an artist I have respected for a long time. Jah Rastafari. *That* is a true poem of who created us all. Jah is why we are sitting here. It's not about making money, about getting your name blasting, about getting your face in the images and places. It's about serving a purpose that is truthful and right.

TED CHUNG: It is really interesting how timing and destiny have worked with this record because it is February, the month of Bob's birthday, Black History Month in the United States, the fiftieth year of Jamaican music and culture— this convergence of things that I did not plan, just manifested themselves and happened. Thanks to whatever higher power. That's the story, certainly, for those of us who had the opportunity to travel with Snoop through his exploration of Jamaican culture, it affected us, and I can only imagine how much an album like this, and a documentary like this . . . will have an impact on the rest of the world, just by the nature of the message we want to project.

[Snoop Enters]

SNOOP: How are you? Did you get here without any weather problems?
BUNNY: No.

SNOOP: Did they tell you what I am doing, Bunny?
BUNNY: I am listening.

SNOOP: Well, you know the kind of music I used to make, right? Thugs. Drugs. Gangbang music? I am pulling away from that. I am on another mission, a mission to do more reggae and things with my music.
BUNNY: You got to do stuff when you got to do stuff.

SNOOP: Through my music, I have found a whole new lifestyle that I feel is close to me. I'm not trying to jump into something I know nothing about, I'm trying to gain full understanding. I don't want to express something that is fake or a phase. It's calling on me. I could have been doing a hundred different things, but I was meant to be out here in Jamaica, to meet you and be part of this music, and to put it in my lifestyle. I want to thank y'all for even giving me the time of day, for hearing me out. I've always had peace in me, and love and unity, the whole Rastafari movement was a part of me, but I never understood it. So, instead of learning about it in America halfway, I figured I'd come out and get it the real way. As I get older and wiser, I'm supposed to say something, but I don't want to jump into it overnight because the brothers, you know, ain't gonna respect that. It's not an overnight success. It's got to be something that's fair to them.
BUNNY: That's real.

SNOOP: Exactly. Because reggae makes people laugh and make babies and have a good time, I always wanted to be associated with it. I also have a lot of love for what y'all did years ago. The Wailers bridged the gap between hip-hop and reggae. I especially want to put a spotlight on guys like yourself, the forefathers.
BUNNY: I think this would be the first time an American is venturing into reggae music and bringing its true message to the world. That, to me, is an accomplishment.

SNOOP: Thank you, Bunny, it's hard. Everybody wants to go somewhere else with it.
BUNNY: I know what you're talking about. I give you credit for trying.

MAXINE: If you promote smoking the weed, then you get it. It fosters communication, community, and creativity between people, not like "Weedgate" in the States. Crack came in and just mashed up the whole place. People stealing from their brothers, their mothers; there was no communal space.

Bunny only uses vegetables
(namely a hollowed-out carrot)
for his chalice, and a pen shaft
for the pipe.

SNOOP: I started selling crack in 1985. When it came to my neighborhood in 1984, we looked at it and didn't know what it was. The next year, everybody started making money; the year after that, homeboys were selling to their mommas, mothers were selling to their kids, girls we loved our whole lives that we could never get with, suddenly we could get 'em with a crumb. You gotta understand, the change put *power* in our hands. It's the wrong kind of power, but still. Travelling through Jamaica has shown me how poor it is. You usually only see the touristy ads, the beaches, et cetera, but it's *poor*. That shit's real.

MAXINE: The same thing happened here: Crack came in, then gangster rap.

SNOOP: When N.W.A. came out they started telling a different story from Public Enemy. Those guys are from Compton, which is right down the street from where I'm from. We didn't say "Fight the Power," we said, "Fuck the Police." There's a difference: "Fight the power, OK, fight the power" [*in a rallying tone*]. "Fuck tha police/ Comin' straight from the under-

"I DON'T WANT TO EXPRESS SOMETHING THAT IS FAKE OR A PHASE. IT'S CALLING ON ME." —SNOOP

ground / Young nigga got it bad 'cause I'm brown / And not the other color so police think / They have the authority to kill a minority. / Fuck that shit, 'cause I ain't the one / For a black mothafucka with a badge and a gun / To be beaten' on, and thrown in jail . . . [*in a hostile tone*]. He's speaking from the experience of having the police beating us, right? A year later, Rodney King gets beat.

BUNNY: My first rap song was a dud. [*Singing, sounds like rap.*] "Ching-a-ling-a-ling, school bell ring, / It's back to school again. / And it's ABC, one, two, three, tic-tac-toe, / And it's all in the road. / So, one, two, buckle my shoe. / Three, four, shut the door. / Five, six, pick up sticks. / Seven, eight, then you lay them straight. / Nine, ten, you go back to school again." ["Back to School Again," a song by the Wailers, later redone by Shabba Ranks.]

SNOOP: Wooo, that was heavy. What year was that?
BUNNY: 1960-something.

"THINGS GET TO YOU, BUT MUSIC CAN TAKE AWAY ALL YOUR PRESSURE AND STRESS. WE ARE THE DOCTORS WHO WILL HEAL THE WORLD WITH MUSIC."

—BUNNY WAILER

SNOOP: God . . . what?
BUNNY: Bunny Wailer did that. Back before you started rapping [*laughs*]. That's mostly what this culture is. Music is a very, very serious part of it. Things get to you, but music can take away all your pressure and stress. We are the doctors who will heal the world with music. Sometimes you're crazy, and it's just the sound of music that takes away the craziness. Ok, so give us the lyrics, give me the song itself and let me go do my homework.

Diplo: Yes, sir. You want to play it real quick? These are the parts I want to confirm with you.
BUNNY: I'll look at it to see what can be done to make it better.

SNOOP: Yes, we love constructive criticism. We don't have any set, locked ideas. You are the great Bunny Wailer. If you feel like you want to flip it, dip it, and whip it . . . hey, man, do what you do.
BUNNY: Yeah, man, I'll be listening first [*laughs. Song begins to play . . . Snoop starts to sing along*]. Give me that rhythm, something.

SNOOP: Play that "No Guns Allowed." [*Lights blunt and music starts. Snoop sings*] "So long, yeah, boulevard / So long, no regrets." We're gonna have a lot of little kids on that record, too. I'm proud of this music right now. I can play it for my mom or my grandmother. I've never been able to perform for them 'cause my music has been like way out-of-pocket [*laughs*].
BUNNY: MMMMMMM [*laughing*]. You're on the right track [*laughing*].

SNOOP: This ain't no gimmick for me.
BUNNY: Yeah, you don't want people to be saying things that aren't true. Records don't matter as long as you're saying the right thing.

SNOOP: And you feel good about what you're saying. Like you said, when you hear your records twenty, thirty years from now, you're supposed to feel great about 'em.
BUNNY: Yeah!

SNOOP: Like I said, I meant those songs, too, that's who I am. I don't feel detached from any of the music I made. It's still me. This is just the growth of a dogg who is becoming a full-grown, wiser man.

During their meeting, Bunny had this to say to Snoop Lion for his introduction to reggae.

Give thanks. It's a pleasure. It's an honor to have Snoop Lion in my face. I've been taking in what you've been doing and I'm saying, "That brother is a lion." Jah b. Bless up. Bless up. We have come down through reincarnations to be who we are now, So give thanks every time. Rastas have to be very close to what is nature, to what is life, so that we can communicate with the power of nature, the power of life, Haile Selassie I. I've been seeing the "I," looking at the visions, the visuals, and the televisions. But to see the eye, It's always a pleasure.

I am Bunny Wailer, and I've been Bunny Wailer since 1962, that's when we met, The Wailers. That's where we started, in Trench Town. You have to go through Trench Town, as a musician, as an artist. We studied Motown with Curtis Mayfield and the Impressions, the Tempta- tions, Otis Redding, all the brothers who came through here who may or may not be with us physically, are forever with us. Bless up, Snoop Lion. Every time. 'Cause I am who I am, Bunny Wailer, survivor of the legendary Wailers— I'm still here doing what the Wailers did from "Simmer Down." That's the first track, and I'm still simmering down. You look like one of my brothers. When this gets old, I'll change the carrot. I'm in here doing these things Because I am a very serious artist and musician focused on making sure that my brothers and sis- ters are awakened. Do the Right Thing. You're a studio man and I'm a studio man and if we look at each other, away from each other, we are still looking at each other in the studio. I miss my brothers Bob and Peter. To be here now is lonesome. I am very satisfied to know that, although I am here, sixty-five years in Babylon, life was not started when sixty-five years got started. There are millions of years that relate to my life. I am still looking forward to the unification of the African people everywhere. Sometimes we are focused on being Africans or white folks or Chinese or Hindu. If you stick my flesh, it's one color that comes out, and pain doesn't have a language. We've all got red. I pray that he learns from the good or the wrong things that he might do.

I vision Bob sometimes, and I vision Peter sometimes, and when I vision these people they are alive. I can speak to them. I can touch them and I can sing with them, playing their guitars. Yes, Lion, it's good to see the man. I'm reggae. Let's keep it reggae, ska, rocksteady, reggae-matic. The music is endless, limitless. When a newborn child cries out, that's music. Reincarnated means that you've been here, and you are going to be here, and you're still here. So lift up thine head and be lifted up to the ever-living doors, and let the king of glory enter. And who is this king of glory? He is the most high, strong, and mighty, the most high and mighty in battle. He is the king of glory. That's the focus. That's the knowledge. That's the way we are.

★ Geejam studios is on the north side of the island in Port Antonio and is co-owned by Jon Baker who was a music industry producer at Island Records. Bunny Wailer came down to Geejam for a recording session with Snoop, which is featured on the *Reincarnated* album. Bunny is pictured above with producer Dre Skull, who, like the DJ Diplodocus Diplo he collaborates with, reaches beyond typical musical boundaries and categories.

When the Power of Lov
Overcomes the Love of Pow
the World Will Know Pea

Resource Project (888)822-7075 www.peaceproject.com (#S328)

The VICE and music crews enjoyed an atmosphere of pure creative po
during long workdays punctuated by studio cat naps: Andrew "Moon" B
middle); Angela Hunte (top right); Jahdan Blakkamoore (middle right);
(from left to right): Andy Capper, Diplo, Suroosh, Dre Skull, Alex Miller,
Ariel Rechtshaid, Snoop, Dre Skull (again), Diplo (again), and Ted Ch
They added their music, smoke, and general chilly chill to the stud
vents and acoustic foam.

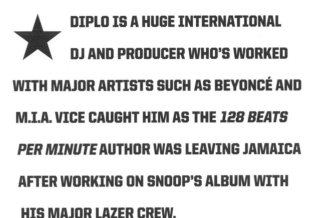

DIPLO IS A HUGE INTERNATIONAL DJ AND PRODUCER WHO'S WORKED WITH MAJOR ARTISTS SUCH AS BEYONCÉ AND M.I.A. VICE CAUGHT HIM AS THE *128 BEATS PER MINUTE* AUTHOR WAS LEAVING JAMAICA AFTER WORKING ON SNOOP'S ALBUM WITH HIS MAJOR LAZER CREW.

VICE: So what's up?
DIPLO: Just doing whatever, being cool and funny, which are two things I can't actually do.

VICE: [*Laughs*]. Yeah.
DIPLO: But I can try. Maybe I can go to cool-and-funny class.

VICE: Try really hard.
DIPLO: Here I go. Let me know when it's ready to roll.

VICE: OK, we're rolling.
DIPLO: I'm Diplo. I didn't sleep last night because I smoked Snoop Dogg's weed till about 7:00 a.m. It's what, 9:45, 10:00? I don't know what time it is right now. We're going to talk about some of the music I enjoy, and I'm going to try and dig up some ideas from the depths of my brain, because I don't even . . . I'm not even awake. First of all, we're in Jamaica. I was introduced recently to an awesome singer named Hollie Cook, the daughter of the Sex Pistols's drummer Paul Cook, and she makes great reggae music. Hers was voted the number one Caribbean album by this website Large-up.com, which is a site I really like and check a lot. The album has a classic kind of vibe, and it's more like roots reggae. Another artist that Suroosh introduced to me last night was Friends and their song "I'm His Girl." I love the video. It's, like, a no-wave New York City kind of vibe.

VICE: What did you like about it? I have a hard time with that group.
DIPLO: The girl performing in the video is so cool. Maybe if I listened to more of them I wouldn't like it, but I like her attitude in particular. I heard they might not be good live, but even if she just looks past the crowd and makes love to the audience, it would be a great show to watch because she has that sexiness and that real cool style everybody's got right now—the high-waisted jean shorts, stuff like that. I'd wear high jean shorts, but—actually I didn't put on clothes. I hope I packed.

VICE: How about the "Nobody Canna Cross It" guy?

DIPLO: That video was pretty funny. It's a Jamaican newsclip about an overflowing river remixed. I like the beat. It was a pretty big success. Another YouTube video that we showed people in the U.S. was a news report of a cow going crazy in the countryside. They actually had to transcribe the guy's words, they were so thick with the country accent here in Jamaica.

VICE: Who else are you a fan of right now?
DIPLO: Kendrick Lamar. He has a new Atlanta-style track beat called "Cartoon & Cereal." He is a rapper from Compton who had a big record that was a hit called "A.D.H.D," which I really liked. The new track is kind of like Dr. Octagon or MF Doom or something real weird. I really like A$AP Rocky, as well. There's a whole new crop of rappers. I think my favorite is Danny Brown. He's a Detroit guy with, like, a crazy haircut. He always wears the craziest fashion. He has a big gap in his teeth and a crazy, high-pitched voice. He has an old-school Public Enemy flow, kind of half screaming, jerking around, acting crazy. He's got a real ghetto sensibility in the raps, and his beats are real good—they're something between J Dilla and Company Flow. He's, like, shock rap. I love when there's a video of A$AP Rocky talking about the beef with Tyler [the Creator], and he's like, "Man, those guys, they fart and burp. We just like to dress cool." They're, like, trying to describe the differences but actually being assholes, yet it's kind of right. Those guys are more about shocking and they're more juvenile. Tyler's voice is one of my favorite rap voices there is—maybe there ever was. I'm not that crazy about the message, but I like what it does for L.A. hip-hop. I love all kinds of rap music, but what's cool about all these new scenes from New York is that they remind me of what I grew up listening to. I was always into *Rap City* and the videos. It would be, like, Black Moon and Smif-n-Wessun, the Artifacts. The intro song was really New York and gritty. The producers who are making this new school of rap, such as Clams Casino, they have that same gritty, low-fi style. It's not about the mix sounds of the records; it's about how nasty they sound. A$AP Rocky's great, though, because he combines everything. His flow is straight up, like Bun B, like New York circa 1996—a cool combination.

VICE: How about Action Bronson?
DIPLO: I love him, too. He sounds so cool, man.

VICE: He sounds so, like, Ghostface Killah.
DIPLO: He's like Ghostface Killah, but I like the way he looks, too. He looks like one of your uncles that you just want to hang out with, the one who's like, fat and cooks, and has a big beard. One of my favorite rappers is Riff Raff, who did a song about Action Bronson. I've done a lot of records with Riff Raff, producing for him, just for fun.

VICE: I didn't know you did Riff Raff.
DIPLO: I produced for him, and, yeah, there are a couple records he put out. He puts up a new video every week, so I have a hard time keeping up with what he makes.

VICE: People are always like, "You've got to sign him. You've got to sign him."
DIPLO: I feel like he could have a hit. He just has no coherence; he is neverending. I wrote a video treatment yesterday, and sent it to him. I

It's very clever. In fact, you should watch my video right now for "Express Yourself" featuring Nicky Da B. It's my favorite song that I made in a long time. I showed it in New Orleans.

VICE: So how's the album for Snoop?
DIPLO: I got two awesome dub plates on this record. I have Snoop Dogg doing "Drop It Like It's Hot." Popcaan doing a tune. And I got Bunny Wailer doing "Simmer Down," which is so cool. He is so cool, man.

VICE: Bunny Wailer's one of the best guys I've ever met.
DIPLO: He was intense, but now, he's my homie. We're emailing and stuff. I'm learning about Rastafari.

VICE: Which is something that you'd consider?
DIPLO: I like the idea of a religion that promotes health because that's pretty rare. I mean, Christianity probably does, too, but no one ever has any respect for that. I like the fact that Rastafari's so steeped in health and well-being in your body. That's really cool.

VICE: How did Popcaan get involved with the album?
DIPLO: He's part of a team I've worked with. Popcaan is like the young up-and-coming dancehall artist everybody loves because his songs are all about parties and girls. He doesn't write any slack lyrics, and he doesn't have a beef with anybody. He has a cool voice, real innocent, and a different attitude—nothing homophobic. He just wants to make people happy and get back to party music again, without having to be, like, gangsta or subversive or anything. He has the biggest records at the moment and is part of Vybz Kartel's crew. When Vybz Kartel was locked up for the five murder charges, Popcaan kind of stepped up and became the spokesperson for that whole Gaza side of Kingston. He's in Guyana in Suriname touring at the moment, and he'll be back on Monday.

VICE: What's his best record?
DIPLO: "Party Shot." He has a video for that. "Get Gal Easy" and, of course, his biggest hit, his introduction song, "Clarks" with Vybz Kartel. "Clarks" is a style of shoes that dancehall guys picked up on that you can buy in a bunch of bootleg colors—in Kingston at the mall. I bought a pair of white ones. I've never worn them; they're just so crazy looking. You'll always see Popcaan—when he came to the studio, all his boys had on Clarks. They had a little toothbrush to clean off the edges. I like that style. They have swag.

VICE: What is it? Is it years and years old?
DIPLO: Yeah, Clarks have been around forever in Jamaica. Any kind of English pretty-boy trend, all the way back to two-tone days, anything that comes from England—that street style comes here, and they kind of take it and flip it. That clean kind of English style, more than the raving cowboy weirdo style that a lot of people do, with the pointy boots and the super-tight jeans and the giant belts with huge belt buckles. Dancehall style is unique. You know what else is funny? All the Rastas love to wear Ed Hardy. Or maybe Ed Hardy's a Rasta.

VICE: I think he is.
DIPLO: I'm going to eat my breakfast.

VICE: OK.

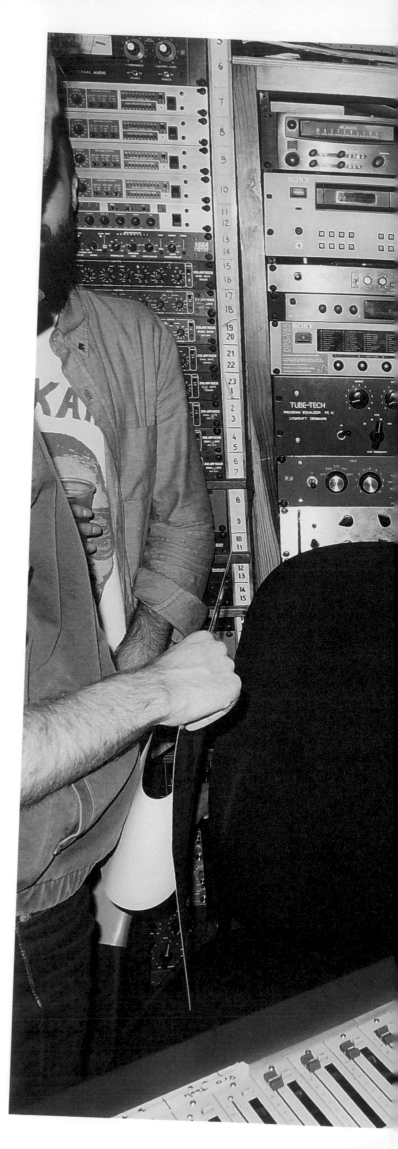

ANGELA
HUNTE

ANGELA HUNTE IS ONE OF THE MAIN WRITERS ON THE *REINCARNATED* ALBUM, PENNING SONGS LIKE "HERE COMES THE KING," "ASHTRAYS AND HEARTBREAKS," AND "NO GUNS ALLOWED." SHE'S WORKED IN THE RAP INDUSTRY FOR A NUMBER OF YEARS, STARTING HER CAREER WITH THE LEGENDARY VIDEO DIRECTOR HYPE WILLIAMS. SHE WON A GRAMMY FOR HER SONG "EMPIRE STATE OF MIND" WHICH WAS MADE FAMOUS BY JAY-Z AND ALICIA KEYS.

VICE: So Who Am I/What's My Name?

ANGELA HUNTE-WISNER: I am Angela Hunte-Wisner from Brooklyn, New York, here in Jamaica as a writer for the Snoop project. I wrote seven songs on the album. There's one called "Here Comes the King," which I wrote when I saw the footage of him being baptized because when you find something spiritual, you find that the king has risen within yourself. I think someone may hear that, and it's, like, you know, a "Pass the Dutchie" type of a vibe. But it's so much bigger than that. There's a lyric in there that says, "You might think you're a lord, but here comes the king." I think that explains what he's going through, what he feels now. He was already great, but now he's even greater.

VICE: Can you talk a bit about your history as a songwriter? We heard you used to be homeless in the early days.

ANGELA: I was homeless, like, right after I started wanting to be a songwriter. People don't understand: We are the main ones, the backbone of the song, but we're the lowest on the totem pole. It takes a long time to become a songwriter who's worth something and during that journey, there's no money. We don't get paid like producers. We don't get up-front money. We don't get any of that. Most songwriters are broke for long, *long* periods of time. If you're really serious about it, you deplete your entire life's savings to do this craft. That left me homeless for a long time, but it didn't stop me from doing what I had to do. I'm from New York. We don't fail.

VICE: And now you've written one of the most famous songs about New York.

ANGELA: We went to the studio that day and wrote what, at the time, we called "New York, New York." We wrote that song in, like, five or ten minutes. Bam, bam, bam, bam, bam! Originally, we were going to do it for someone else, then I was sort of joking, saying, "Why don't we send this to Jay-Z? It's really cool, it's New York. We're talking about the city, and the resilience of New Yorkers. Why not send it to him?" So we sent it out. We got an email back saying that he hated it, and we were like, "OK, we kind of figured that. Let's just move on." So we moved on and sent the song around to different places and, a couple months later, Big Jon [Platt] my publisher at EMI, who is extraordinary at what he does, was at a barbecue with us and heard it. He was immediately like, "I gotta get this to Jay, he needs to hear it!" I was like, "It's already been taken." We sat there for the next two or three hours while he tried everything to get me to give it to him. After a week of going back and forth, we said, "OK." Then Jay-Z heard it and loved it and recorded it the next day. At the time it was me on the record, then he suggested we should get Alicia [Keys]. We all agreed someone else should be on it and tossed around some names, Mary J. Blige was one of them, but Jay had already done a record with her, and he'd never done one with Alicia, she was from New York, and we have the same type of tone in our voices. It all worked out and the rest is history. It's one of the songs I'm most proud of.

VICE: How would you describe Snoop to people who just know the gangsta thing; the surface sometimes people don't look past?

ANGELA: Snoop reminds me of B.I.G. Biggie was hysterical. Women were in love with B.I.G. because women love a man who makes them laugh—despite what everybody thinks, you know, the gangster this and that. Where we come from, that shit's survival. Nobody wants to be a drug dealer, it's something you're forced to do. He wasn't like that because he wanted to be like that. Are there people like that? Yeah. But the majority of them? No. Snoop is a good person, and I've always known him to be a good person. He has a very big heart. He's brought us all here, not knowing if we could deliver or if he was gonna get what he wanted. He doesn't know most of us here, and he took a chance and that says a lot about him and trust, which is rare in this business. He consistently talks about how he can't do this or that without the team. The team, the team, the team. That is so foreign to me. The music business is an egocentric "I" type of thing. It's amazing to hear someone say how much he appreciates every single person here, from the managers and the film crews and security, to all the people who are making us breakfast every morning. It's the reason this project will work—because everyone has a role and everyone has the highest respect for everyone else's role. One of Snoop's catchphrases is "Teamwork equals dream work."

VICE: That's what he said to me when I said, "Can you get in a hot-air balloon, and we'll film you." He said, "Hell, no! You get in the hot-air balloon; I'll do the voice-over, 'Teamwork equals dream work.'"

ANGELA: Ha! Yes. When you 're surrounded by that, how could you not have an amazing project? Snoop knows that. I'm happy to be a part of it. Actually, I'm more than happy to be a part of it. I hope that the documenting of it will show how much everyone's giving. I've bitten off a piece of my soul and put it into every song I've written so far, which I hope, in turn, will make a very soulful record.

CHRIS
BLACKWELL

CHRIS BLACKWELL WAS THE MAN RESPONSIBLE FOR BRINGING BOB MARLEY AND THE WAILERS' MUSIC TO THE INTERNATIONAL STAGE WHEN HE SIGNED THEM TO HIS INDIE LABEL, ISLAND RECORDS. SNOOP RAN INTO THE LEGENDARY MOGUL WHILE STAYING AT HIS RESORT NEAR KINGSTON, STRAWBERRY HILL. THE TWO HAD THE FOLLOWING CONVERSATION, WHICH WAS NOT SEEN IN *REINCARNATED*.

SNOOP: How are you, Mr. Blackwell?
CHRIS BLACKWELL: Very well.

SNOOP: Pleasure to meet you, brother.
CHRIS: Pleasure to meet you, too. Good to see you in Jamaica.

SNOOP: Happy to be here. It's a different kind of experience for me this time, too.
CHRIS: First time?

SNOOP: No, I've been here before, but usually when I come, I just stay in a hotel room for the show or concert. I've never experienced Jamaica like I did this time . . . the Maroons, the Nyabinghi temple. I got a chance to meet you and stay at Strawberry Hill. I'm just doing it big. I'm actually baptized in the Rastafari spirit right now. I got renamed and everything. My new name is Berhane.
CHRIS: Really?

SNOOP: Yes.
CHRIS: When somebody told me what you were doing—I said listen, you already were, like, Rasta. Inherently. Because Rasta is free spirit and you're a free spirit.

SNOOP: That's what the Rastas told me.
CHRIS: You're also one hundred percent unemployable, like me.

SNOOP: They told me that you discovered Rastafari when your boat crashed and you swam and they brought you back. Is that true?
CHRIS: Yeah, it's true. It's hazy now, but just over there . . . it's too hazy here for the cameras, but right over there, at that time, there was nothing.

SNOOP: No mountains, no city?
CHRIS: The mountains were there, but the city . . . there were no people living there at all. The story I gave out was that the boat broke down, but in truth, I ran out of gas.

SNOOP: So you had to go swimming to get some more gas.
CHRIS: We managed to paddle the boat—me and a couple of others. We paddled the boat inland, then it was too dark to go anywhere. There was nothing, nothing. It was, like, swamp, so we slept on the ground in the swamp. I got up at six in the morning and said, "Look, I'll go and see if I can find something." I walked for hours and hours and hours, alone through swamps on the side of the coast.

SNOOP: You were swimming?
CHRIS: No. Walking, and sometimes swimming 'cause I didn't want to go inland. I felt if I stayed on the shore, at least I wouldn't get lost.

SNOOP: You'd be safe.
CHRIS: Exactly. And, literally, it was about two or something in the afternoon, and I thought I was going to die of thirst. I came into a little clearing, and there was a hut. I called out to the hut. This Rasta put his head out the window. Now, this was the early '50s, when everyone, of all complexions, was against Rastas.

SNOOP: They were, like, the outlaws, right?
CHRIS: Exactly. There was a lot of negative press about Rastas at the time, and so when I saw this guy, I was terrified.

SNOOP: You thought he was going to get you 'cause of the press that was put out against them. [*By the 1950s, Rastafari's message of racial pride and unity had unnerved the ruling class of Jamaica, and confrontations between the poor black Rastas and middle-class police were common. Many Rastas were beaten, and some killed. Others were humiliated by having their sacred dreadlocks cut off. In 1954, the Pinnacle commune was destroyed by Jamaican authorities.*]
CHRIS: Exactly. However, since I was dying of thirst, I asked him, "Do you have any water?" and he said, "Yeah," and brought me some water. He was so gentle, and so sweet in how he did it. I was just like, "I'm so exhausted, may I lie down somewhere?" And he said, "Yeah, come in." There was, like, a palette on the floor, just off the ground. I lied down there and fell asleep. This must have been about three in the afternoon, and when I woke up, night had fallen and there were seven other Rastas in this little hut. I was scared, really scared.

SNOOP: You thought you were about to become dinner.
CHRIS: Exactly. But when I woke up, they chatted with me, read to me from the Bible, then a couple of them took me back.

[*Not long after this experience, in 1958, Blackwell released a recording of a blind jazz musician named Lance Hayward he discovered while teaching water skiing in Montego Bay. After a few successful recordings on his fledgling indie label, Island Records, he was able to make enough money to set up offices in the U.K., acquiring rights to more successful Jamaican acts.*]

SNOOP: And that gave you a newfound respect.
CHRIS: Yes. And, of course, a lot of musicians were Rastas. Because with Rasta, you basically have to be a carpenter or a fisherman or a musician because those were the only jobs they could get as societal outcasts.

SNOOP: Something you can do with your hands.

"YOU SAW THE STAR POWER IN THEM BEFORE THEY WERE STARS. THE STAR POWER AND THE STIGMA."
—SNOOP

CHRIS: When Bob [Marley] and Peter [Tosh] and Bunny [Wailer] walked into my office, which was in London, they were stranded there. They were broke. They didn't have anywhere to go or any money to get back to Kingston 'cause the person who'd brought them over hadn't given them return fare. I tell you, they walked in like princes, these guys. It's one thing to be charismatic if you're . . . if everybody knows your name and they see you on TV, but it's another thing if you're busted. They were like princes. Even though Rastas had a bad reputation at the time, I had a positive connection to them because of my experience in the jungle.

SNOOP: You saw the star power in them before they were stars. The star power and the stigma.
CHRIS: Before I signed them, they were stars in Jamaica. But what happened is that they got a bad reputation in the music industry there, which they broke away from because it was very corrupt at that time. So they started their own label, Wailing Souls. They made their own records, but then couldn't get them on the radio.

SNOOP: The payola was real heavy over here.
CHRIS: Yeah, it was barely legal. I mean, it's illegal everywhere, but then no one gets around that way. That's why some time back in Jamaican music, in my opinion, payola went down a little bit because everyone in the music business . . . they were all gangsters. Musicians were singing about what was going on with the system, and how they were not helping the people, and the oppression that was happening within the country. The government was not doing anything to have the people at peace with them so the musicians who were Rastas were singing about all that and showing the world the real face of the leaders of the country. So. . . who else are you going to visit while you're here?

SNOOP: Bunny Wailer. His storytelling ability is awesome.
CHRIS: He's incredible.

SNOOP: When the Wailers first brought you music, did you know it was going to end up being classic music or did you need to put your thang on it to make it that way?
CHRIS: When I met them in England, I felt like I really wanted to work with these guys, but they had worked with a lot of people and it hadn't really worked out. I thought, you know, the key is trust. So I felt that I should trust them. I asked them how much it would cost to do an album. They said four thousand pounds—or whatever it was. So I wrote out a check for four thousand pounds. I gave it to them and said, "Go ahead and make it, and I'll be down in Jamaica in a couple of months to hear how it's going." Everyone said, "You're so crazy. You're never gonna see a dime when you go out to Jamaica."

SNOOP: Like, they were gonna run off with your money, right?
CHRIS: Yes. So I came back down to Jamaica, they picked me up, and took me to the studio and played me what became "Catch a Fire."

SNOOP: Mmmmm!
CHRIS: I couldn't believe it. It was one of the highest points in my life. At the time, reggae had a reputation in England for being novelty music. It wasn't considered serious and I felt, you know . . .

SNOOP: That they deserved more respect than that.
CHRIS: And my image was how to break them, as a Black group, as a Black rock group.

SNOOP: Not even reggae but just as a Black rock group so that people could look past the fact that they were making reggae music.
CHRIS: The first record . . . when it was finished, I said "This record is incredible. This is one of the best records we've put out. We're gonna sell a million of them." I remember I was on the road with Traffic, a band I worked with a lot, and I rang back the office to see how the record was selling. This was about three months after it came out. I talked to the guy and he said, "It sold six thousand." I said, "Six thousand? That's all it sold?" And he said, "Well, that's good for a reggae record." I was so pissed. His head was still in "It's a reggae record." I was pissed. But anyhow, eventually it sold. Millions.

SNOOP: So the Wailers were basically all evenly talented but Bob knew how to orchestrate it and keep it all together, right?
CHRIS: I think they were all too strong to stay together. That was the problem. And also, Bunny didn't want to tour. I brought them over to England and it started to snow and, boom, Bunny got on a plane and left. When you see him, you should ask him about it. He got on a plane and left. So, there was a time there when it was just a stalemate.

SNOOP: So you had to take Bob and go solo? Because y'all worked together so well and he got it; he understood the theory of pushing and promoting.
CHRIS: Right. And I think he got it. You know what I mean, what I said about being a rock group. I'm not sure the others . . .

SNOOP: They wanted to stay in that lane. He knew about the growth; he understood that he had to take it out of here to take it where it needed to be.
CHRIS: Yes. So I was saying, "Forget about that." I told them, "You're never gonna have a hit in the Black charts in America because Black America isn't interested." Black America was just getting into Jazz and knew nothing about Caribbean or Reggae music. The U.K. was much more receptive. The Wailers also looked like a rock band, which I had been signing a lot of. I wanted to turn them into another rock group, but with a reggae twist.

SNOOP: They wouldn't accept reggae music like that. Black America wouldn't accept reggae music as Black music.
CHRIS: Well, they definitely didn't at the time. Things changed, though.

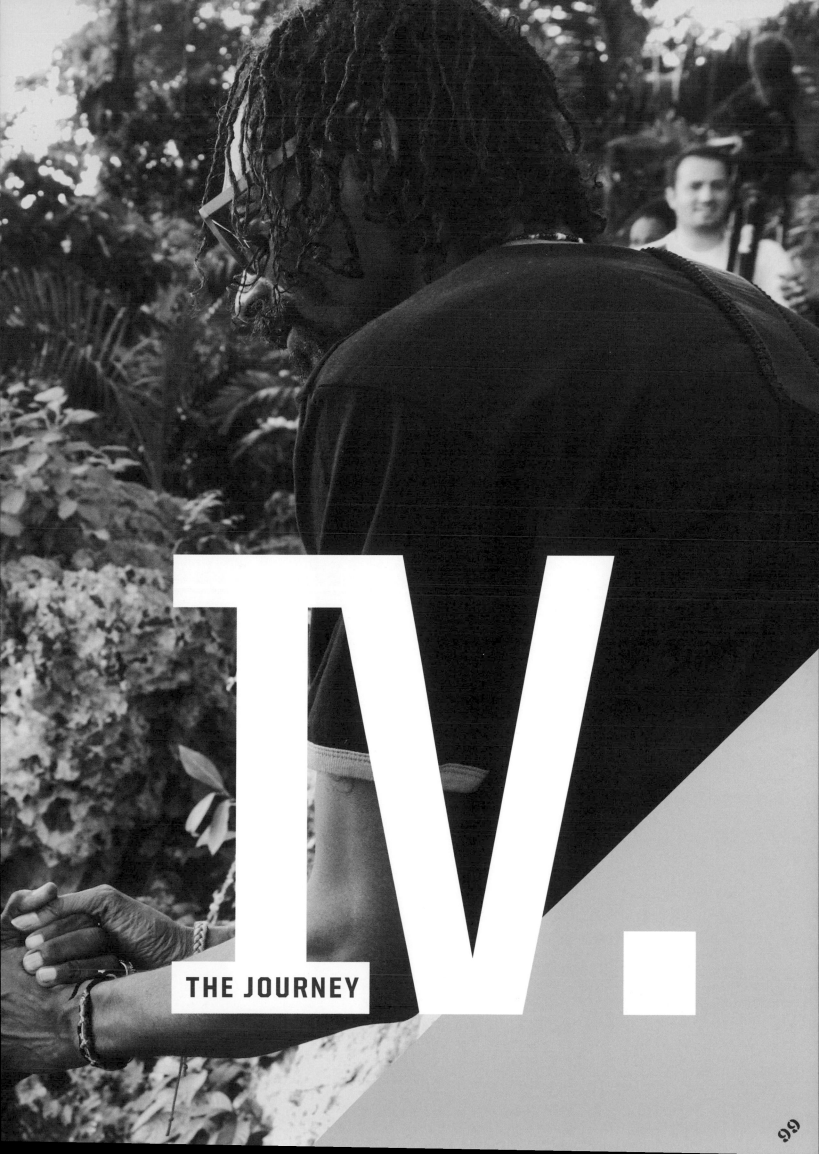

IV.

THE JOURNEY

Charles Town is the home of the historical Maroons, descendants of Jamaican slaves who, in the eighteenth century, fled from their masters into the hills on the island, where they formed their own communities. Today's Maroons still stick to the traditions that were left to them by their forefathers. Their community is self-sustaining. For the most part, they live off the land, venturing into town only to obtain items they cannot grow themselves. They are a very private group of people who normally do not allow outsiders into their community, which made our visit a special privilege and an unprecedented filming opportunity.

NANNY OF
THE MAROONS

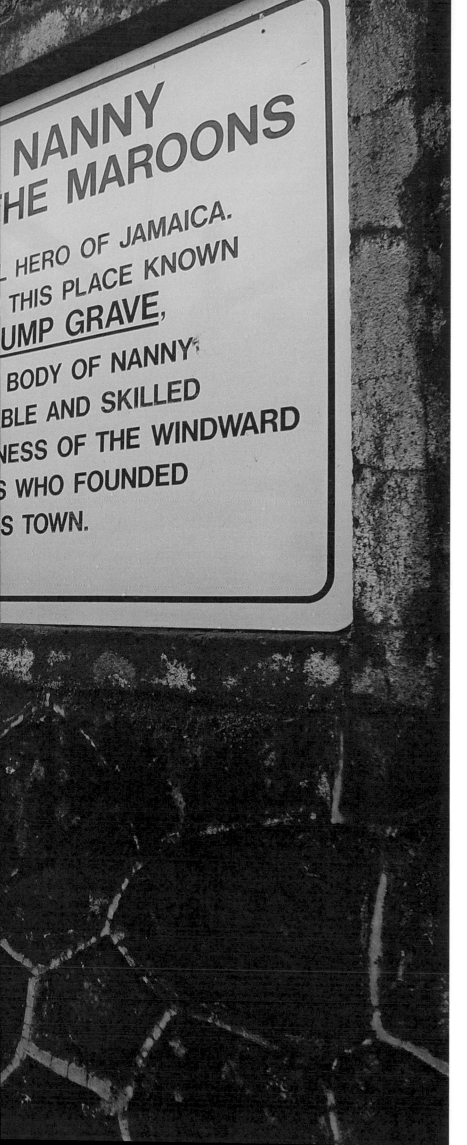

NANNY
THE MAROONS

L HERO OF JAMAICA.
THIS PLACE KNOWN
UMP GRAVE,

BODY OF NANNY
BLE AND SKILLED
NESS OF THE WINDWARD
S WHO FOUNDED
S TOWN.

Nanny of the Maroons was a slave who still remains the only female Jamaican national hero. Born in Ghana in 1686, she was sold into western slavery as a young woman and was celebrated for her decision to flee after severe mistreatment. When she and several other slaves escaped from their plantation and settled in the Blue Mountains, members of the military tried (but failed) to hunt them down. After their escape, their

settlement remained a haven for other escaped slaves and their descendants continue to thrive today. The exact nature and date of Nanny's death remains a mystery. Many believe she died of old age, but due to the clandestine nature of the Maroons community, no historical records have been able to confirm this. It was important for Snoop to visit the Maroons, who have inspired and influenced many reggae musicians in Jamaica, and to connect with a people known for their resilience and core values in the face of great odds.

The community held a celebration in honor of Snoop's visit and taught him the dance of the Maroons and the beats of their drums. Though they have been branded rebels (even in modern Jamaican society), the Maroons are very pious Christians.

NYABINGHI TEMPLE

THE TEACHINGS OF
S MAJESTY

Nyabinghi is a branch of the Rastafari movement that considers Haile Selassie I, who was emperor of Ethiopia from 1930-1974 and heir to a dynasty that has traced its roots back to King Solomon and Queen Makeda, the queen of Sheba, to be the son of God brought down to Earth.

We visited the Nyabinghi temple, funded and built by Bob Marley, to bring Snoop closer to the spirit of Rastafari. Snoop's love of reggae and Bob's cultural engagement with the Rasta community made it a good fit for an introduction to the elders of the Nyabinghi order.

"I HEARD A VOICE, HE SAID THAT I WOULD UNDERSTAND. / ONE KING ONE FAITH ONE RELIGION. / IF YOU LOVE ME COME AND JOIN THE REVOLUTION."

—SNOOP LION, "HERE COMES THE KING"

We were granted access to this group (who have never been filmed, not even by local media) who customized a "Binghi" celebration to welcome Snoop as part of the Rasta family. Upon meeting the elders, we fell in love with their style of dreads and dress. They baptized Snoop as one of their own and renamed him "Berhane," meaning, "Light" which, unbeknownst to anyone at the time, was Bob Marley's baptized Rasta name (or Ethiopian Orthodox, according to Rita Marley's site).

H.I.M. Haile Selassie I

The Nyabinghis have a huge tapestry of Haile Selassie I hanging in their temple. "Rastafari" comes from his name before he was crowned king: *Ras Tafari*, composed of *ras* meaning "head," and *tafari* which is a man who is to be feared, a hero. Rastafari believe that Haile Selassie I, the former and final "Emperor of Ethiopia" is another incarnation of the Christian god (along with Christ), called Jah.

The Rastas invited Snoop to share their chalice and showed him how they prepare it. "Wisdom weed," or "holy herb," is very important to the Rastas. Smoking it is considered a communal sacrament during which the smoke acts to purify the body, clear one's mind so that it is freed from the establishment and the truth is easier to see, and bring the soul closer to god. Rastas cite many Biblical passages that support herb used this way.

Shante, Snoop's wife, was there for this critical moment for Snoop. After leaving the ceremony, she fully realized that his journey was not for show, but instead something spiritual and life changing.

120

Snoop wanted to have another meeting with the elders of the Nyabinghi order and invited them up to Geejam for a reasoning.

V. LIFE AS LION

LIGHTERS UP

"BOW"
—SNOOP

WORLD PREMIERE

⭐ *Reincarnated* got accepted into the
Toronto International Film Festival
in September of 2012. Snoop was moved once
again, as he relived moments in the movie
that were very personal and touching to him.
He was in a state of euphoria watching with
everyone else, getting the reaction of the
audience, even though he had seen the film
before. Getting into festivals and the positive
critical reception were bonuses of an already
awesome experience for all of us.

The high priest of the Nyabinghi Ras, George Ion, being filmed by our Deputy Producer, Will Fairman.

ACKNOWLEDGEMENT

This journey is inspired by my wife Shante and dedicated to my beautiful family: Spank, Lil Snoop, and Cori B.

Jah! Rastafari!

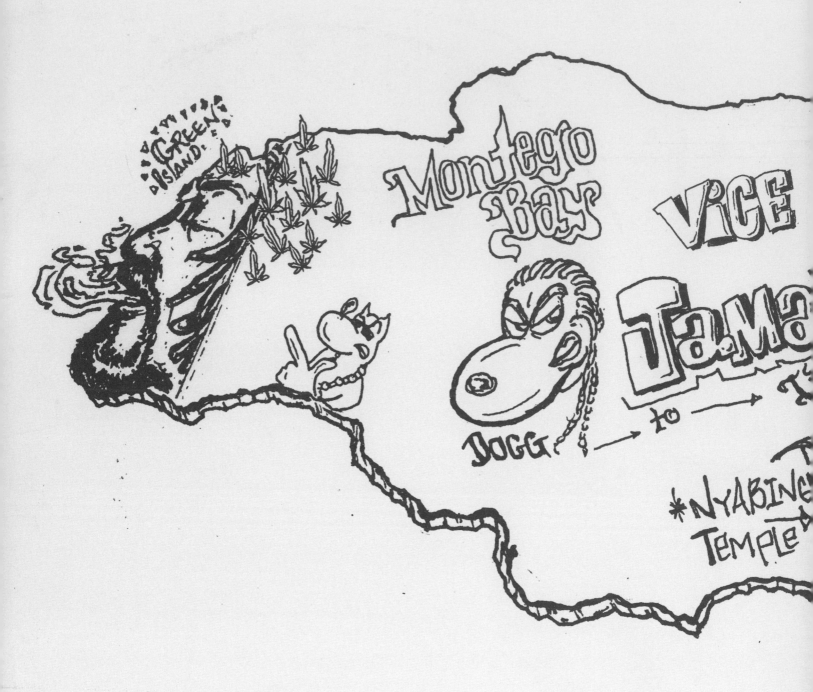